SOUL SPEAKING

AMY BRETALL

**OPENING THE WAY to SPIRITUAL INSIGHT
LIVE YOUR INSPIRATION**

Copyright © 2025 Amy Bretall
All rights reserved.
Published by Arbor Grove
amybretall.com

ISBN-13:
978-1-7358226-6-2

No part of this book may be reproduced or transmitted in any form or by any means, electronic or mechanical, including photocopying, recording, or any information storage and retrieval system, without permission in writing from the author.

All Scripture quotations are taken from The Holy Bible, Revised Standard Version of the Bible, copyright © 1946 and 1952 the Division of Christian Education of the National Council of the Churches of Christ in the United States of America. Used by permission. All rights reserved.

All definitions are taken from Webster's Ninth New Collegiate Dictionary, Copyright © 1990 by Merriam-Webster Inc.

Printed in the United States of America

To our soul speaking inner spirit and connection to the Holy Spirit opening and leading the way.

Also by Amy Bretall

In Plain Sight: Faith Is In The Everyday

Sights of Faith: The Cross and Clouds

*In Plain Sight Volume II:
Finding Extraordinary Faith In Ordinary Days*

Contents

Introduction & About / 1

Doors Open..4-9
Inner Light / 4
Ideas Need Life / 6
It's Starting Again / 8

Windows & Archways Invites........................10-21
Active Faith / 12
We Are Who We Become / 14
Faith Even When / 16
Softening Spirit / 18
Is Your Faith In Focus? / 20

Steps & Stairways Advance...........................22-29
And Then What? / 24
Do I Move You? / 26
The Up / 28

Bridges to Move..30-35
Connecting Moves / 32
Reflective Perspective / 34

Inspiration & Inner Spirit..................................36
The Light Within / 37
Opening The Door / 47
Our Soul Knows / 51

Develop Your Spiritual Relationship..................55
   Step 1: Prayer / 58
   Step 2: Stillness / 73

Step 3: Gratitude / 77
Step 4: Bible / 83
Step 5: Scripture / 91

Spiritual Insight..**97**

Divine Guidance..**105**
From the Heart / 107

Natural Movement......................................**108-117**
Faithful in the Smalls / 110
Believe It / 112
A Rising Voice / 114
Letting Go to Move Forward / 116

Benches for Rest...**118-129**
Rest Brings Restoration / 120
There's Always a Bright Spot / 122
Bench Nook in Four Seasons / 124-127
Take Your Shot / 128

Closing with Openings...............................**130-142**
Contrast /130
Opening A Way / 132
Repeating Patterns / 134
Narrow Focus / 136
A Lens of Faith / 138
Will You Bring Out Your Idea? / 140
His Sight. Our Insight. / 142

My Faith Background / 143
Photo Locations / 144
Acknowledgments / 145
About Author / 147

Introduction

I didn't plan on this book. I didn't plan to do anything with these photos, but that's how all my photo books evolved—over time a pattern appears in the images and stirs me from within. On morning walks I'm moved to take capture things I find beautiful. Some photos speak to my soul. I feel them. My inner spirit says "Ooh." Thus, the title of this book is *Soul Speaking*. Our spirit informs.

I began curating this collection of photos, my spiritual eye drawn to them, before I knew I was starting another book. While organizing these pictures, a larger overarching theme of movement appeared: doors, windows, archways, stairs, benches, and bridges. It was unknown, unseen, until focusing upon; clarity the outcome of reflection. All of the objects in the photos symbolize movement with layers of meaning. All taken in while I was in motion, walking, pausing to capture the view. Move in order to be moved.

Seeing the pattern, I became spiritually moved to focus a book on our inner spirit, the influence of our spiritual relationship, where our inspiration comes from and the formation of ideas. I kept going deeper. It's how the Holy Spirit moves us. It's how I'm drawn to images. They speak to my soul. I write what I see in photos or the message tied to what I experience, realize, and learn. We can be moved by what is innately known within—internal to external.

Our soul, our inner spirit, has a voice. Do you hear yours? Do you know yours? Are you attuned? As we take steps to find it, hear it, be true to it, and take steps of faith, we chart a new path. When we connect with the higher, bigger power of the Holy Spirit, our soul comes alive and speaks. It's divine direction.

Organized and About

Soul Speaking is a hybrid book comprised of 1) photo devotionals: paired pages of photos with aligned writing, and 2) chapters of writing as a standard book contains. The chapters are placed in the middle. Both follow the overarching theme of movement throughout — how we are moved within, with our ideas, how we are moved spiritually –internally to then be moved externally. Chapters go deeper with my personal story to illustrate key points. To apply in your life, practical steps are shared for why and how to develop and deepen your spiritual relationship as a pathway to spiritual insight.

In the photo collection, the theme of movement is reflected within the objects: Doors, archways, and windows symbolize openings of an idea, seeing opportunities ahead. Steps and stairways reflect the work and effort required to gain movement, an elevated point of view. Benches for needed rest, a break of motion. Bridges as a conduit to continue moving, the advancement forward. All synced with the backdrop of seasons gracefully demonstrating a natural leading of change — movement in order to grow. Included within the chapters are several photos of behind-the-scenes images to further the message. These photos are placed on the left side of the page (creative liberty), where the paired devotional images are on the right.

This book is written for your heart and soul. *Soul Speaking* connects our inward knowing to our outward sight. Being connected to the Holy Spirit moves us forward, first through our internal spirit, then through our external movement of action. It's what I've discovered and learned through my personal experience over the last twelve years as I've grown my personal, spiritual relationship and moved forward with an idea. Journey through this book at a leisurely pace, pausing to reflect on each page to let the words and photos speak to you or read more as your spirit-to-mind leads.

About The Photos

The predominance of photos were taken in Kansas City, Missouri. Many are on the grounds of The Nelson-Atkins Museum of Art. I lived near and it was one of my morning walk routes. The outdoor sculpture garden renewed me, not just from the grand artwork, but more so for the lesser-known aspects people may pass by and miss.

Catching my attention are repeating lines, patterns, and contrasts of light. This photography collection of movement formed over a period of four years without realizing it. I'm inherently drawn to objects that show openings, a leading forward, with an implied element of required action. Doors, windows, archways, stairways, benches, bridges, and natural formations. Movement upon our initiative. The curation also features nature with a constant of trees.

The photos are taken in the morning, what I consider the best time of day. The lighting is welcoming, warm, and gentle with an invigorating quality marking the open possibilities.

Importance of images: Photos help us see meaning, something we may have initially overlooked. Images are helpful learning tools aiding recollection and when paired with written message provides context for deeper connection. A combined photo + message helps retain and recall key points. With visuals, we often can more clearly see significance. Spiritually, we have inner perception. There is subconscious power in what our eyes consume — images are collected within our mind's eye, staying and informing us even when not consciously apparent of the message. To the eye of the beholder: Exceptional photos evoke feeling, leave a lasting impression, ignite inspiration, and can speak into our soul.

I hope these photos and writings stir your spirit into movement – from the inner to the outer.

Inner Light

It's easy to not. The hard part of anything is in the doing.

Ideas and opinions are easy. It's the implementation and execution taking the effort— in mindset and "timeset." The doing is work, and sometimes it's extra hard or takes longer. And you better bet, when you do something for God, the Devil of Doubt lurks around to pull you off your path. That's where a developed and disciplined *personal* relationship with God comes in. The sweet spot of faith lies within —your inner thinking, your belief, your internal fortitude—your spirit. From the Holy Spirit. An inner faith must exist to counteract the negative shadows of doubt.

A deepening inner faith is the key. It's not what's outside, the external, the going, the doing. It's what's inside, internal—the inner light. What do you feed your thoughts? What's your inner dialogue? Do you keep the negative chants alive? Your thoughts are the key to opening the door of faith. And the great part is, it's within your control. They are *your* thoughts.

A personal relationship with God, honed through prayer, attuned to your spiritual self, ushers the way. Make no mistake, you have to take the action. Ask, seek, knock, open, walk. You don't get to borrow faith. You don't get to skip over the building of faith muscles.

The secret sauce of faith is the inner reward—steadfast prayer, taking steps in faith, standing in your faith when no one is around, and soaking in the sweetness of God's goodness which will show up in small, wonderful ways.

Let your light shine. | Winter
"Ask and it will be given to you; seek and you will find;
knock and the door will be opened to you." Matthew 7:7

Ideas Need Life

Creativity needs space to think and grow. If all you have in your head are a bunch of ideas you don't take action on, at some point they clog up mind space, prevent new ideas from forming, and/or die off. Ideas need life.

Not moving on the creative energy of an idea, the spark, is a restriction. If you hold back on that one idea then what happens the next time you have one? You've already set an internal limit. And it's a lot easier to not take action, once again, because you're already stuck. Your spirit feels it and informs the brain. "Oh, right, this person isn't going to let it out." You have to take action on it for more creativity to flow.

Creativity through our ideas is an energy source within. Hold back on it and you'll feel it. You may not even recognize the signs; we often aren't attuned to the spiritual side of mind/body/spirit. Creativity comes from our spirit—our own uniqueness that bubbles up and seeks to be released.

Train your brain to act. That's you. How long will you wait? How long will you think about it? Years? The what if. The what could "it" be? The idea inside—it's for you to bring out and give it life.

Don't wait for a grand opening. Create it. Open the door. Use your creative energy and as you use it, more will come.

Will you open the door?
Does a door need to be closed so you can move forward? | Winter

It's Starting Again

The innate movement of ideas organizing in the mind and the instinct to *do*.

Moving up from within our spirit, formed within our heart. Implementing ideas brings forward future ideas. It's a natural cycling of stored energy. Flow is born from doing. An object in motion stays in motion, Issac Newton taught.

To move forward on an idea takes confidence. Doing is the catalyst for developing confidence. Doing generates the ability to overcome doubt, which invariably creeps in. Then when you've taken action once; you can do it again. Doing → Confidence → Doing → Courage.

Inspiration moving within. Acting upon ideas to implement. Flow is another outcome when we consistently do, act, take steps. And it's starting *again*. What happens if we don't move on that idea? It stops. No movement. No progress. No advancing to the next phase. We also learned from Newton's Law of Motion an object at rest stays at rest. Overcome inertia and utilize internal energy—inspiration and ideas.

We uncover ideas within us by developing our spiritual relationship. Spiritual vitality applies gentle pressure within causing us to move. This spiritual strength is a moving force. It *compels* us forward. We *want* to. We *have to do* because it's uniquely within us. Move according to the purpose set in you. "We know that in everything God works for good with those who love him, who are called according to his purpose." Romans 8:28

"It takes courage to grow up and become who you really are."
-E.E. Cummings, American poet, author (1894-1962)

The light within is your spirit.
Bring your light out to share with others. | Spring

Doors, Archways, Windows

All represent openings, showing a way forward, the opportunity ahead if we see them, take initiative, and move through them.

Doors, windows and archways can also represent the opposite—the contrast of not. Not moving forward, not being open, not taking an opening made for us, keeping it closed, stuck in the status-quo, shutting out the what-can-be, not having our eyes directed forward. Perhaps even looking back, holding onto what once was. To grow in life we can't hold onto things in our past. Whether it's the story we tell ourselves, a prior hurt, or wanting something gone.

Like Scripture says: Don't look back. Our spiritual direction is to move forward. It takes courage to do so when we don't know what's on the other side— that's called faith.

Openings ahead.
Photo left leads to this window view.

Active Faith

It's amazing what faith can do in our lives. It gets us from here to there. It can take us to places we never imagined.

From an emotional state to a knowing state. From knowing to believing. From a low to a leveled high. From frustration to peace. From internal to external—how we show up to the external world comes from within our spirit. From inaction to a state of purposeful doing and not stopping. To being moved to act, bringing out our inherent, God-given talents and gifts.

Active faith has an energy. It stirs within our spirit, our heart, and wants out. It's linked to our natural creativity, being an energy source of ideas. To be expressed. To be shared. To help others.

Active faith moves within—our spirit is connected to the Holy Spirit. We feel it. We may feel it before knowing it. For optimal spiritual health our soul likes movement—growing, deepening, learning—through daily, faithful disciplines. This internal spiritual growth is then shown externally through our actions. Active inner faith causes momentum. Being moved spiritually starts from within.

About the Photo, right: I didn't know the garden cat was near and that she stepped into the shot. A cat has a mind of its own. I didn't want her in my photo, but like it. Timed quite nicely. Takeaways can sometimes be hard to see. In the present, timing doesn't always work to our advantage. We prefer to have control. I could not have queued up the cat if I wanted to. It's like our spiritual relationship. We ask, want, wish, work towards, and pray for certain outcomes, but many things we have no control over in life. It's helpful to believe in God's set-up. Timed by the Spirit. Queued up just right. Thank you.

Change your view and your view changes. | Autumn

We Are Who We Become

We are who we become.
We are the will we choose.
The inner work shaping to form.
The environment of talk and our own.
What do you say to yourself?
What do you believe?
It starts from your inner voice.
Talking yourself in or talking yourself out—the balance of sway leans.
What feeds that voice?
Will you listen to faith?
Whose voice do you listen to?
Your voice is a measure of your will.
Do you have the will to speak your voice?
Will you speak the voice of your idea?

We are who we *allow* ourselves to become.

We become through change.

Definition: Become (verb): To come into existence, to come to be. To undergo change or development.

Stepping into what's yours to do.
Do you see your opening? | Autumn

Faith Even When

Faith is for every day of the week. Not every other day. Not faith tomorrow. Not just on Sundays.

It's a developed discipline so you'll have faith when things don't go your way. When your client doesn't pay or your employer lays you off. When your child takes a misstep. When your "till death do us part" departs. When your orderly life plan didn't take your orders.

It's faith when.

How do you have faith on the road ahead when you aren't sure and you don't see the path? A foundation of faith sets our focus, our tone, to be in hope, see the bigger picture and be at peace within. The space is our spirit.

It's using your time — this time, this day, every day — to develop faith. Practice it to make faith a habit. Pray. Read the Bible. Get in stillness and listen. Feed your mind spiritual content. Memorize Scripture. Recite verses. So when you're tested or hit with a challenging situation, you'll have a strong foundation of support.

When faith is *within*, you have faith *even when*.

"What no eye has seen, nor ear heard, nor the heart of man conceived, what God has prepared for those who love him, God has revealed to us through the Spirit." 1 Corinthians 2:9-10

Window photos shown are from the inside looking out.
Our inward is how we view outward.

Softening Spirit

I relate to this hard straight line of the window because I've been hardened from a few bigger life letdowns and low-downs. At times I've wanted to hold onto that hard edge. That hard line can be a defense mechanism. It can protect.

But I've learned to soften. How? By deepening my personal faith relationship helps. Depending on faith for my life focus and how I choose to spend the short time of life helps. Time in stillness to think, reflect and become self-aware is helpful. I'm always learning. I don't have it all figured out even though my tough side, the "Suck it Up Buttercup," wants to. I embrace the gentle side, the softer side for a balance.

Age also has a way of softening if we use our years of experience to reflect, learn, and apply to gain wisdom. Purpose has a way of softening, while also doubling down. Softening, but not stopping. Softening, but not lessening the focus and resolve.

So, while I enjoyed the hard edge to this window (it pleased my eye, photo right), I hung curtains, softening the line. "Amy, do not be afraid." I had to give it up. And you know what? I like it even better now. There's a new softness, replacing the hardness. That's what our spiritual connection, our faith relationship, does too. It takes the edge off. It can fine-tune and soothe those hard lines we may want to keep.

An upside to the downsides of life is who we choose to become. What we get through. What we learn. It's ours to assimilate. No one can take away our internal thinking, our inner being, our inner spirit and our faith belief.

"Create in me a clean heart, O God, and put a new and right spirit within me." Psalm 51:10

"The eye is the lamp of the body. So, if your eye is sound, your whole body will be full of light;" Matthew 6:22

Is Your Faith In Focus?

Choosing a faith mindset instead of doubt and worry is a daily choice. It brings spiritual balance.

Reading a chapter in the Bible every morning sets the tone for the day. Not later in the day, not sometime during the day or evening, but as a start. It helps to keep a faithful focus and reframes our mind to remove any external, negative influences.

I call this "faith-setting"—holding a faith-focused mindset above all else. It involves shifting our perspective and filtering the distractions in order to see the bigger, higher life picture. How we interpret external circumstances and challenges beyond our control determines the quality of our life experience. Life really is *how* we *see* things. To adjust our view, we often need a faith filter in order to view the situation differently.

Renew the mind and recharge spiritually to see anew. Keep your faith in focus.

"Do not be conformed to this world but be transformed by the renewal of your mind, that you may prove what is the will of God, what is good and acceptable and perfect." Romans 12:2

What we look upon grows.

Steps and Stairways to Advance

Stairs and steps hold a compelling pattern and symbolic meaning. Stairways are a visual for reaching goals through effort.

The forward motion, a simple repeated action to reach your mark. You will rise. Step by step through effort. You will move forward. Gaining an elevated viewpoint from the work. It takes consistency. Sometimes it takes longer as that staircase extends—oh, the end isn't right there? It has a steeper incline than initially noticed — that happens when on a new path. Or it has those tricky narrow little steps that make it harder to navigate. Have you encountered that?

The great companion on those steps is your faith. With faith, there's no escalator to replace the steps of doing— the time, the inward turning, the spiritual disciplines, your belief. No one else can give it to you. It's what you make it. You can't borrow faith from your parents or friends— it's yours to develop. Once you start, it grows! What's grown my faith the most is when I've taken steps in faith.

When I've fallen in life, faith helps me stand. It's that handrail, right there, within reach to help. It is support to rise again and move forward. We just have to reach for it and take steps. Is your faith in reach? What steps are you taking?

Step by step. Faith helps keep the pace.

And Then What?

What are you going to do once you've gotten to where you think you should be?

If you believe 'Life is in the doing,' then mesh, mash and massage it all together— your gifts, your skills and go for it! Sure, there is risk. How much are you willing to take? It's for you to define the scale and set the value.

My mind says practical things like you should make more, save more. Will I have enough? Is my future secure? Then my inner voice, my spirit, reminds me of my real job, to be faithful and obedient, and that lets me be sure in how I spend my time.

I will do what I've promised. In any relationship, if I say I will, then I will. I won't alter my word because of external factors.

And now, I will take this "risk"—it's a better angle than looking back wondering "what if?" That's a perspective I'm not willing to take.

And because my promise is to God, I trust the outcome, whatever that may be. I'll trust His plan.

The depth of our faith determines the ability to step out and take a risk. Who is the risk for? If we have faith in what God has given us, then shouldn't we be willing to trust and obey? Is the view of risk real? It lies in our internal capacity to move out of our self-imposed limitations, out of our cushy comfort zone of control, and overcome uncertainty with the belief of our developed faith. A *developed* faith to a *deepened* faith to a *depended* upon faith.

"Keep steady my steps according to thy promise, and let no iniquity get dominion over me." Psalm 119:133

An invitation to advance, forward movement. | Spring

Do I Move You?

Do I move you? That's what the Holy Spirit wants to do. To move within us. To move us. Moved to act. Moved to share. Moved to help. Moved internally is the first *step* to then be moved externally— from here to there. Where God is leading?

Moving on our ideas, stepping through the opening we see, stepping out on faith leads to insight. Clarity can often be known from within, before our mind understands the full scope of meaning.

This photo moved me. Spoke to me. It *is* something. But what? Opening the spiritual mind's eye is inward knowing to our outward sight. Our inner voice to outer expression. Our internal inspiration and ideas to external implementation of action.

Symbolism and seeing: Layers of it in this photo taken at dawn. Are you stepping up and through? Do you see your opening? Divine guidance with a lighted way ahead. Stairway to heaven. The stark contrast of light and dark in the early morning. The definition of dawn (verb) is to begin to be perceived or understood; to begin to grow light as the sun rises; to begin to appear.

God leaves nuggets on our path. Do we have spiritual insight to recognize them? It can be received by visible sight. Other times it's an internal prompting, a knowing from within. Developing our spiritual relationship opens the way to insight— what our inner self knows, by what The Holy Spirit gives to us.

"Remember not the former things, nor consider the things of old. Behold, I am doing a new thing; now it springs forth, do you not perceive it? I will make a way in the wilderness and rivers in the desert." Isaiah 43:18-19

It's a new dawn. Step up, greet it, get it.
Rising within and rising above. | Summer

The Up

Stairs. Leading forward, moving upward, new elevations, above where we are now, an invitation to advance.

From this place of here to the space of there— spiritually focused to be spiritually moved.

Don't underestimate the Up. When I used to bicycle, riding up a long ascent, I would say to myself "Up, up Amy," while focusing on the pedal stroke up, the up motion. Not just the down stroke, which inherently exerts more dominant muscle strength from the quadriceps to press into. On hills, it helps to utilize the upstroke to incorporate the hamstring muscles. The pulling motion of the up, using all of our sources of power.

It's similar with faith. We often think we are the dominant, sole force moving ourselves through life. But if we turn to the Spirit, it can move us more powerfully. It is the greatest muscle force to be developed. There is power in the spiritual Up.

"Take up the shield of faith..." Ephesians. 6:16
"Get up! Pick up your mat..." John 5:8
"Stand up. I am only a man myself." Acts 10:26

Have you tried to power through life on your own accord? Harness your spiritual energy within for a powerful lift.

Where will that idea lead? | Spring

Bridges Mirror the Movement of Ideas

Bridges connect the gap, a conduit to the next, from here to there, opening a way, keeping us moving over barriers.

A way forward. Keeping the movement of ideas and progress, to the next.

Sometimes we need a stepping segue to move into the next. I'm here and I feel led to go there. It's steps of faith to bridge the gap. It's always steps upon steps, pathways and segue that get us over the hump, a conduit for continuing movement, and onto the next.

Bridges also have strategically placed lights along the way to help us. God does that too, with little signs, nudges and nuggets. We often take the sights, the lights, the signs for granted. Pay attention to his lights along the way.

Sometimes it's nice to have a visual representation—bridges help make this point. Keep taking steps and bridge your faith from here to there. What keeps you moving?

Creative energy speaks through and to our soul. | Autumn

Connecting Moves

We all start somewhere.

Before I had the idea of a book, let alone a series, I had my blog and photos. And before I had a blog, I wrote and posted on social media. And before I wrote about faith, I wrote about My Sweet Jean, a dear friend of twenty-two years, 45 years my elder, who I lovingly refer to as my adopted grandmother. In 2015 I began writing and sharing about my love for Jean and what I was learning during her rapid health decline. Sharing helped me handle her soon-to-be passing.

Reflecting on my faith journey, I now realize Jean was a bridge. She bridged the gap from writing about her to writing about faith. Bridges serve a purpose and take us from where we are, to where we are going. Sometimes we don't recognize the connecting moves until years later. That's the function of a well-designed bridge — it naturally flows and moves you forward. Often by divine guidance.

Will you continue and finish what's been started in you? Reflect to see your connecting moves.

"For I know the plans I have for you, says the Lord, plans for welfare and not for evil, to give you a future and a hope." Jeremiah 29:11

Full Circle | Autumn

Reflective Perspective

Photos can provide a perspective into reflection.

Do you take time to reflect? What is reflection? To think and go deeper, to develop an ability to see our circumstances and understand the true situation, not for what we want, but for how it is.

Reflection can also be gained after years. Time shows a pattern, if we stop and notice, to synthesize. Hind*sight* brings clarity if we choose to see. Others can help us to recognize our *blind* spots, broadening our perspective. "Ah, yes, I didn't realize that—I didn't see it from that angle. Yes, that now makes sense."

"The spirit of man is the lamp of the Lord, searching all his innermost parts." Proverbs 20:27

What we think about is a reflection of our spirit. | Summer

Don't underestimate small beginnings.
It's how God gets us started.
Before books, before gallery shows, I had photo cards (2016).

The Light Within

I first heard my soul speak when I was in the process of turning my photos of crosses into greeting cards. As in, the actual putting them together. I printed 4"x6" actual photos and placed them into precut cardstock, specifically designed for photography. It was a time-consuming process to make. Additionally, I hand-signed the back of each one. Not a standard, generic card, but a keepsake gift. I'm sharing the backstory because it's the first time I felt spiritually alive. Do you know that feeling? The sensation of your soul being lit from within?

It's how I discovered a new energy source — being spiritually alive. From our spirit. A standard wellness, well-being, framework is "mind, body, and spirit," but it's the spirit that takes priority and should hold the top spot. Our inner spirit is an instigating, initiating, generating energy source that begins internally, then moves us externally. Informed by the spirit, action flows to the mind and then our body responds. Spirit to mind to body.

How I found my light within, and the heightened awareness of my spirit, is best shown through one of my early writings. Before books, I had a blog. This also highlights a principle of how starting with one small idea can progress, evolve, and grow into more than imagined.

Sharing how I became aware of this new energy source, the power of our spirit. I had been writing for several years, then in January of 2017, I started a blog. This was my second post:

Spiritually Alive

What does it take for us as adults to feel alive? Not just happy. Or content. Or at peace. But *Alive*?

I've felt *physically Alive* after cycling 102 miles or when I hung with the pack on a 50-mile road race. That was a feeling of physical aliveness. I feel *mentally Alive* when I have pushed myself to learn something new, expand my mind, doing a mental task I've never done. Last year I read a 1,087 paged book for pleasure (small print), the longest book I've read. Or a greater mental accomplishment I completed was the discipline for ten months to read Og Mandino's Scrolls three times per day— morning, noon and night.

But an even more important aspect I discovered recently is the feeling of *being Alive* in my soul. What I found while working on a creative project to help a young girl I met in Cuba, I was following my heart, being led by faith, pursuing the cross, I found the feeling of Alive.

I was inspired to help someone. And for months, little by little, spending time over photos, from a starting point of an idea, asking, not knowing, seeking, exploring, being frustrated, having road blocks, keeping going, persevering, and taking time. Somewhere in the midway point of this project, my spiritual journey growing, my dining room table was covered in photos, prints, papers, ideas, I had the bubbling up of a new feeling — it was the sense of being Alive. My soul and spirit talking to me, a soft assurance that bubbled up: Amy, Alive. What a discovery because this was one of my three words that spoke to me in January 2016: Live, Breathe, Alive. Yes, I'm finding

You. No more hiding. This action brings me a feeling of my soul and spirit being ALIVE. From the inner to the outer to shine. "This little light of mine, I'm gonna let it shine." I am trying to fully shine. Maybe I'm feeling this more because I've been selfish in life. Yes, I've helped people in my twenty-year human resources career. Sure, I've donated money to charities, volunteered my time at non-profits and given my time and skills through numerous community boards. But, what did I, Amy, solely do, act upon, to create something of value, to help another?

I've learned it takes us pushing our own self to feel the power of Alive. It takes us following faith, helping others, doing something to make a difference with nothing asked in return for our spirit and soul to come alive.

Do you know spiritual aliveness? What makes you feel alive? What are you doing to make your spirit come alive?

Inspiration Is From Within

I started because I was inspired to help a girl I met in Cuba. That's all. There was no intent to do anything more. Not gallery shows, not books. Simply, my motivating factor was to help someone.

The backstory of why I created the cards is necessary to illustrate a significant point in our spiritual development —it's from within.

Being inspired comes from within us. In-spire. It's from within. It's connected to our spirit. Why we take action is dependent on the strength of our internal, spiritual relationship. It's our why. It's what moves us internally and then externally to work it, to bring it out, to share it, in order to help others. The definition of inspire brings meaning.

Definition: Inspire (verb) Latin: In + spirare = to breathe [more at spirit]. To influence, move, or guide by divine or supernatural inspiration. 1b: to spur on (motivate). 2: to breathe or blow into or upon. 3: to draw forth or bring out. 4: inhale.

The definition of inspire points us to the breath, a divine influence, something that moves us, to breathe. It connects further the point of something within, linking also to spirit, from Latin origination. Our spiritual relationship is like oxygen. A life-force to inhale, an influence to aspire. To bring out, to breathe upon, from what is within us. Further interest is the definition of inspiration supporting the linkage to our spiritual relationship and divine connection.

Definition: Inspiration (noun) A divine influence or action on a person believed to qualify him to receive and communicate sacred revelation. 1b: the action or power of moving the intellect or emotions. 1c: the act of influencing or suggesting opinions. 2: the act of drawing in; specifically, the drawing of air into the lungs. 3a: the quality or state of being inspired.

Inspiration is a natural and authentic movement.

If you never bring an idea out, and work on it, it's suffocated. It will die off. Will you feel it within your body? An idea connected to your spirit and the Holy Spirit, you will. It's the opposit of being spirtually alive and invigorating. It's draining.

We all have a light within us waiting. Wanting to be found and ignited. It only takes a spark to set a fire ablaze. We can give it the air required and breathe life by "doing" the idea. The air is our spiritual relationship, what we feed our soul.

What lights you up? I didn't know this "lit" me up, or was within me, until I took action and made progress on the first idea. It takes work to find it, however there is a natural leading from our spirit. It was in me. I couldn't not do it. It was six months of working, doing the little steps, figuring out details, moving it forward, before I *felt* it and knew was my spirit coming alive. Still today, I remember the exact moment. Sitting at the dining room table that was covered with materials. The actual photo cards coming together, I was making the final product, where I had the overwhelming sensation of being spiritually alive. Key point: We have to uncover in order to discover.

What is the light within you? What does your inner voice speak? Are you listening? Do you hear your *Soul Speaking*? How do you nourish your spirit?

"Let your light so shine before men, that they may see your good works and give glory to your Father who is in heaven." Matthew 5:16

"breathed into his nostrils the breath of life;" and man became a living being." Genesis 2:7

Inspiration Required

Being inspired to help someone was required for me to take action. Why? Because there is no way would I have done all the work it took to produce the photo cards.

If it was just for me, my own self-interest, I would have given up after a few months. I would not have pushed through all the small pain points that were frustrating to stumble upon. It was annoying to keep finding little things to figure out. So many small steps to just create an idea, a product to sell as the vehicle to help the girl and her family. It takes more brain power to do something new, something you don't know. It's not like I was using any of my expertise from my twenty-years in human resources. I had no background for pixels, color sources for prints, designing the back layout of the card, etc. Each step had to be researched and that took time. I share this point in humble spirit, not to point to the work it took, but to the persistence to overcome.

My spirit was led. Two years prior to this point in time I was deepening my personal, internal spiritual relationship. I started praying to God. We formed a relationship. I connected to something higher, bigger. This is how our spirit, connected to the Holy Spirit works. First, we are moved internally, then we are moved externally.

Spiritual Energy

Before my first book, I thought I could continue with my usual business work. That I could just sit and stay in my safe harbor, career comfort zone. I tried to just set "it" aside, but a part of me was dying inside. The idea, and my spirit, was suffocating. Then when I'd return to work the idea, I felt alive— spiritually alive. It's an energy form like no other. It leads you. It moves you.

From a financial standpoint, it would have been advantageous to remain focused on my core career income. Again, it's how the Spirit guides and can moves us when we follow. Even for monetary gain, my soul spoke and I kept moving towards it, not away from it.

So, when I tried to set this aside, I felt it internally. Intensely. Why? Because I had already let "it" out. I let my spiritual energy and ideas flow, sharing photos of crosses and writing about faith on social media for several years. In the beginning, and for years, it was more as a hobby and side project. I called it a passion project. But it took hold. It was "in" me. It had roots from being worked on, watered, tended, weeded, and pruned. My spirit grew. I dedicated more time on it. Feeding it, nourishing my soul, when I worked on it.

Keeping things in doesn't feel good. Held back, held down, held in, instead of a natural release. Like pent up emotions that aren't shared, get stored in our body and are negatively felt. Something held in is called repressed. Not letting it out prevents our natural form of development to take place. It's the same with an idea. What is within us needs to flow out. Our inner spirit has an innate need for freedom, to be expressed, not repressed. Key point: Don't hold back on what God gives you to think about. What bubbles up from within you. It's our spirit, our inner voice. From within us. Holding in and not moving on that first idea, the trap is set, preventing, not allowing, more to flow.

"If we live by the Spirit, let us also walk by the Spirit." Galatians" 5:25

Spiritual Movement

One of Newton's Laws is an object won't change its motion unless a force acts on it. We are the object. What is our catalyst? An underestimated powerful force for moving us is our spiritual motion. It's what goes on within us and the connection to a higher, bigger influence of the Holy Spirit.

Our spirit, connected to the Holy Spirit, is the spark to overcome a physical state of inertia. Inertia is the tendency to do nothing or remain unchanged. What gets us moving? What gets us to take action on an idea?

God plants a unique light, a spark, within each of us. It's up to us to develop our faith, through a spiritual relationship, connect with the Holy Spirit to have the confidence and courage to find it, work it, and share it to help others. All to the glory of God.

Spiritual is a state of being. Being spiritually alive is from within us. It's an energy. Listen to the energy source because it gives and depletes. Our "it" of an idea wants out. The living Spirit makes us feel alive.

The more we invest in our spiritual health and connection with God (the spirit within us via the Holy Spirit) the deeper our connection to our soul. And it just might become your sole purpose. Soul to sole.

Spiritual Transitions and Seasons

Nature leaves clues. Like seasons (the photos accompanying this book are included to illustrate this point further), there are times for transitions and letting go in order to move forward. It's needed to grow.

<u>Back to the storyline</u>: For four years I sent care packages to the young girl (her name is Yordielis, she was 11 at the time we met), and family through her mother. We kept in contact during this time through social media, exchanging messages.

Mailing packages to Cuba, a communist country isn't routine, nor inexpensive. There is an embargo; the United States Postal Service and US companies do not deliver. I found a way through a connection I just happened to meet. At that time, it would cost $120-150 to mail a medium size box. That cost on top of the contents of the package itself, small gifts, U.S. items that teen girls like, American candies, jewelry and hair accessories, and mainly over-the-counter medicine they could not access. Initially, I gave a lot of thought to the contents, but after a few years realized it really didn't matter the extent of the things sent. The bigger point of the package was delivering hope. Hope and acts of kindness are powerful.

Even when I translated the messages in Spanish each time, there was a language barrier. They did not speak English. During the time of our communication, I took two in-person college Spanish courses, in the evening, to learn more and refresh my long ago high school Spanish.

Over time the relationship changed and then faded. It became harder to remain connected.

What I was able to offer wasn't enough. There were unmet expectations for more. I prayed intently about it and how to handle. That's the thing about spiritual insight, God will give it to us when we develop a direct relationship with him. My spirit was leading me and I knew what I had to do. I had to let the relationship go. It's not an action I took lightly, but knew it was the right one. Over the years, I pray about her and know if God wants me to do something again, he will inform me. There will be clarity.

Here's what I've realized through reflection and prayer. First, sometimes the people God blends into our life are not forever. Some seasons are shorter than others. The lesson is for us to recognize when it's time to let go in order to move forward.

Secondly, God blended her into my life to get me started. Yordielis served an important purpose as my inspiration to do something with my cross photos, turning them into cards. I would not have done it for just myself, it was way too much work. While putting this book together, reflecting on the purpose of bridges and my progressive steps taken over the years, it's only now that I clearly see this new angle. God knew it too. She was a bridge to move me forward. I needed a why, a bigger reason, to do the work. My why was to help her. Bridges connect us from where we are, to where we are going, keeping the movement. Refer to the Bridge section for more.

<u>Storyline and about the cards</u>: People did buy the photo card gifts, but it didn't cover the costs of the care packages. That reason didn't factor into the consideration process as I still sent them. Due to the time involved to handcraft each card, it wasn't scalable, nor profitable. It was what a local business owner told me: "Cards are hard." Hallmark, a Kansas City, Missouri-based business, doesn't primarily sell cards any longer, they sell gifts and more.

"This little light of mine, I'm going to let it shine," from the children's gospel song, written in the 1920s by Dixon Loes.

Opening The Door

Our starting steps literally "open the door" to our spirit. Letting ideas and inner knowing emerge is freeing. No longer trapped within.

Taking action on our ideas is a literal escape latch. If I didn't start with the initial idea to turn my photos into greeting cards, I never would have had the flowing following: ideas for prints, gallery shows, to seeing new images to capture, and writing. Like me, in the beginning you may not even realize you are "starting" something. Initially, I was moved to take photos of crosses without even consciously knowing it.

Creative expression of our internal ideas needs an opening. Getting connected to our spiritual health— our faith relationship—is a gateway. It's how we can discover our innate ideas and creative talents. I only found mine by tuning into my spiritual side by deepening my faith with prayer. I listened within. Connected with *my* spirit *and* the Holy Spirit moved me first internally and then externally. What are you moved to do?

Opening Ideas: What Can They Become?

We have to work the idea and take action to bring life into it— to breathe into. Just thinking about it, talking about it, wondering is not enough. Why? Like opinions, ideas are easy. Everyone has them. It's easy to think something. It's another to implement an idea and work it through the process.

What helps this "breathing" process? Our spiritual side— faith. It takes steps of faith to bring it into existence—to live. To become Alive.

Today, and only now as I prepare and organize this book, bringing connection points together to share this evolving process and story to help others, I find a deeper connection to three words that bubbled up from within me ten years prior. Three little words my spirit held. Three little words that rose to the surface in a significant way. I clung to them. They guided me. Those three little words were Live, Breathe, Alive. Starting a new year, January of 2016, I woke to these words. Coming off several hard years, I was still at a low point and tired. As a recap, two years prior, I turned to my faith as a comfort and for the first time focused on developing my own personal faith relationship and prayed.

Jump forward in time to the current. Last year as I'm reading the Bible a new verse jumps out, a word connects deeper, drawing me in. Amos 5:4, "Seek me and *live.*" It's one of my guiding words, Live, spoke out on the page in a spirit-knowing, soul-stirring meaningful way. "Hey, that's what I did!" I kept seeking God, expressing it through taking photos of crosses, it moved me to see a different perspective and I was living. I became spiritually alive.

"Seek me and live." Amos 5:4

God Grows It

<u>Back to the storyline</u>: So, I had the cards to help the girl. As I continued to deepen my personal, spiritual relationship, the initial idea expanded. One day while praying I had an internal knowing of a new statement, a direction: "Get more crosses in the world." What? I say to God, "Oh, come on? What does this even mean?"

The root of my work has always been photos of crosses. Initially I took the photos of them subconsciously. When starting, it was a natural extension to use my photos of crosses and turn them into cards. I had the photos already and was drawn to them, they pulled me in. I kept looking them. Taking these beginning steps of faith with an idea for greeting cards, making the product, and selling the cards, it came alive.

Here's another cool part of how God grows us and expands our initial vision and thinking. By taking action on that first idea (you can also call this obedience), I then started seeing something new. I refer to them as Everyday Crosses, crosses that are formed in the unformed, see page 142 for an example. I took photos of these too because they were so significant and special to me. Timed and uniquely placed, I received each as a sign, a message telling me "Keep going, Amy. I see you." Like all my photos, I never planned to do anything with the Everyday Crosses. I didn't know I would see so many of them that they would become a beacon. I had to turn them into a book, my first, titled *In Plain Sight: Faith Is In The Everyday*.

I couldn't have planned it. That's how cool God is. See how he works? He is a big picture planner and designer. He gets us moving in the right direction. He places nuggets on our path. Will we pick them up? Will we follow?

So, to get more crosses in the world, over the next few years, I showed my photography collections at various organizations, being selected as a Now Showing artist as part of the ArtsKC program. Then I had two featured, solo gallery shows in Kansas City, Missouri. In addition to The Cross Collection, The Cuba Collection (of crosses), I had The Rural Collection (from my grandparents' farm), and then my capstone debut of The Everyday Cross Collection. This was also a way to validate my photography work since I was new to this artistic arena.

"So neither he who plants nor he who waters is anything, but only God who gives the growth." 1 Corinthians 3:7

Vibrant spiritual health is knowing your soul speaking voice. Knowing your spirit and being connected to the Holy Spirit. It's your personal relationship with God. It's knowing his voice. Following it can bring forward deeper meaning and purpose.

The more we invest in developing our spiritual health and connection with God, the spirit within us via the Holy Spirit, the deeper our connection to our soul becomes. We hear our *Soul Speaking*.

An outcome is a sustaining spiritual energy. It's a living, breathing cycle of developing to discover, deepening to renew, depending upon to make decisions in life and to follow. The Holy Spirit is a power source. Have you tapped into it?

Key point: Taking action leads to more awareness and insight. When we work an idea, it naturally expands. Why? Because God grows it. It's true what is said, "You have to step out on faith, in order to find out."

Our Soul Knows

I didn't know how, but early on, when I printed and framed a few of my photos in a larger size, my inner voice assuredly said: "I'm going to have a gallery show one day." (See page 46 of this poster)

Why did this thought even enter my mind? I don't have an arts degree. Photography wasn't a hobby nor interest of mine. I haven't taken photography classes, nor read about the subject to learn.

When I took the photos, I didn't have any plans to do anything with them. I mean, why would I? I don't even have a professional camera. Then and still today, I use my iPhone to take photos. My education, training and background is human resources and business. So, why would I even think of having a gallery show?
It's what our soul knows. We just have to get connected to it. My inner spirit was waking up and speaking.

Key point: Turning a few of my photos of crosses into greeting cards, to help a young girl in Cuba, was a starting point. Only when

I completed that first step — taking action on an idea — doing the work to develop a tangible product, was I then able to bring forward additional ideas. Progress is a stacking process. We do steps one, two three, before steps four, five, six are apparent.

In this case, I went to a locally owned gift shop in Kansas City and spoke to the owner about selling my card in his store. He told me cards were a hard product to sell because the margin is low and many people want to purchase cards for one dollar. My photography art cards were keepsake gifts. He suggested I print them in larger sizes and frame them. I took his advice and did. That's when I my soul spoke even louder.

Are you connected to your spirit to know it? Are you listening within? Do you hear your soul speaking?

Spiritual Insight

Insight is to get the message. In-Sight. It's an inner seeing and knowing that comes from our spirit. *In*-sight.

To accomplish this, we turn inward. From our developed spiritual relationship, we intuitively know or we take time to think about it. Reflection is deeper thinking. If unaware, in prayer we ask God. "God, help me to know what this means?" It may come the next morning or weeks later.

You may be familiar with the saying "The eyes are the window to the soul," from William Shakespeare, an English playwrite and poet (1564-1616). Similar Scripture is, "The eye is the lamp of the body. So, if your eye is sound, your whole body will be full of light;" Mathew 6:22.

<u>Definition: Insight</u>: (noun) The power or act of seeing into or understanding a situation. 2. the act or result of apprehending the inner nature of things or of seeing intuitively.

Using our senses— from our spirit — we can feel it, hear it, see it. Spiritual insight is an inward knowing. The heart and spirit perceive it, which is a knowing within. We develop this spiritual connection through prayer, our belief, disciplines, and how we live in the world.

Being connected to the Holy Spirit: The concept of the Holy Spirit can be elusive or hard to grasp even when reading it in the Bible. Why? Like belief, it's intangible. It only becomes concrete when we develop the connection through spiritual habits. We grow spiritual insight by taking action and following when led by the Spirit. This is harder than it seems. In theory, it sounds simple, but in application, more is required. It's easy to *say* you have faith. Well, what about when you are being led in a different direction? Will you do it when it's not your plan?

When going deeper to understand concepts, I find it helpful to know definitions. I'm also a word person and want to check if my understanding of a word is the literal meaning. Following this, a synonym for spiritual insight used in religious context is discernment. A related word and synonym for discernment is acumen, meaning keenness and depth of perception. Notice how these words relate to visual reference, the ability to see things? Seeing into, seeing intuitively, and depth of perception. Insight is helping us to see, to understand, the bigger picture, as God intends.

More on this topic of spiritual insight is included later in this book, page 97.

Spiritual Knowing Takeaways:

• Spiritual knowing comes from spiritual being. Insight is an inner knowing.

• Our spirit grows when we take action upon the spark of an idea, the spiritual nudge.

• Not working on our "it" of an idea, not following through on the inner prompting, will produce a block. You'll feel it, but might not recognize it. Our spirit is an energy. It is reduced when you aren't being authentic to who you are and what you are meant to do.

• Ignore your inner spiritual knowing, that voice within calling, and after time it will be silent. You've trained it. Ideas need life. Don't take action and it dries up. You've closed the door, shutting out your inner spirit.

• Our soul, our inner spirit, has a voice. Do you hear yours? Do you know yours? Are you attuned? As we take steps to find it, hear it, be true to it and take steps of faith we chart a new path. When we connect with the higher, bigger power of the Holy Spirit, our soul comes alive— we hear our *Soul Speaking*.

Develop Your Spiritual Relationship

Like all other things in life, we get what we put into it. A strong marriage, a healthy body, a learning mind, you do the work. Because readers are from a wide cross section: those newer to faith to long-time believers, those who don't go to church and those who do, I've included the "why" we should implement these spiritual disciplines (habits). It's what I've personally learned.

This is a practical "how-to" guide to develop and deepen your personal, internal spiritual relationship – your faith. All five steps (habits to implement) are required as a foundation for spiritual insight. It's not a pick and choose menu. If you want just a "little" faith, then just do a little. However, if you are newer to faith or interested in expanding your spiritual side, start with the first step and add additional steps over time. That's a good approach for starting.

If you are serious and want a big, robust, fill-me-up, overflowing, blow-your-mind kind of spiritual life that gives you new meaning and fulfillment, then you do all steps. You go all in. The choice is yours. I'm sharing these 5 Steps in hindsight. My spiritual relationship started with the first step and grew over several years.

We learn best by doing. A key point of this book is just that —doing. Implementing the steps, incorporating them into daily life. It may seem like a hard approach, but here's the cool thing about faith.

When you develop your spiritual relationship and then deepen it to gain spiritual insight, your heart naturally leads you. You are pulled. You are spiritually moved. Your inner spirit gets connected to the Holy Spirit and naturally moves you. You want to *do*.

These are the steps I personally took. I learned the impact and outcomes by implementation and experience. The good 'ole learn by doing. I didn't research what theologians recommend and compile a common list. These steps are Bible-based and rooted in Scripture.

These are small steps, habits, that accumulate and compound into big internal changes when applied consistently. These are all simple actions. It's personal accountability to form the habits, the disciplines, to develop our spiritual health. Spirit to mind to body.

These steps are focused on our internal, personal, spiritual relationship. This is all on your solo time. It's not in a group, not with your spouse, partner or friend. Not in a community of others. It's you. It's your internal spiritual space. It's your time alone to develop these habits. Why? Because it's how we connect deeper with God, personally, one-to-one (1:1). It's an internal relationship through our spirit and connection with the Holy Spirit. It's real. There is a higher power source, that is God.

Throughout this writing I refer to our spiritual relationship with interchangeable terms to include spiritual health, spiritual side, spiritual relationship and faith relationship. To make the point, I often state: personal, internal, individual, 1:1, spiritual relationship. Get the point? It's within us. Not external practices or group worship in church. This is singularly focused on you and your time. These steps are disciplines, habits, practices, getting into a routine specifically designed to connect us with our spirit and the Holy Spirit. The outcome is spiritual strength and is a foundation that will open the way to spiritual insight.

As I've developed my faith, what has moved me most is the spiritual alone time. If you attend church, it can be easy to think a service covers your spiritual health. But church is external — it's going, it's a group dynamic.

Our spiritual relationship requires alone time, personal, 1:1 connection, with a focus on "being" for internal knowing. Yes, you can find spiritual renewal at church, but it doesn't replace the necessity of our own solo time. I know this because I grew up going to church and missed the internal focus. I also know I'm not alone. I struggle connecting in an enclosed space of organized, structured religion. I'm much better at my one-to-one time because I feel the immediate results, the uplift, the renewal. I'm not against church. I routinely listen to sermons from pastors, but it is not the staple, nor a precondition for a developed, deepened and rewarding faith relationship.

I speak from experience because this is what I did and the outcome is a series of faith-based books to help others find faith in the everyday and to grow in their personal relationship with God. As I grew my personal faith relationship, I started seeing crosses and took photos with no intent to do anything with them. It was the entry level leading as my heart and spirit were connecting to a higher power, the Holy Spirit. Ahead are the steps I took. They helped me and I'm sharing what I've learned so they can help you too. In fact, these 5 steps, coupled with obedience, transformed my life.

There are layers and leveling up in our spiritual habits as we deepen our faith. I'm sharing with you the steps I took so you can apply the principles in your life to help you form a spiritual starting place or considerations to add or elevate yours. Small actions done with consistency have big impact in our lives. It's easily overlooked because people gravitate to the "I want to do something big. This is going to be epic." But God starts in the smalls. Do you know what is said about faith starting the size of a mustard seed?

"It is like a grain of mustard seed, which, when sown upon the ground, is the smallest of all the seeds on earth; yet when it is sown it grows up and becomes the greatest of all shrubs, and puts forth large branches, so that the birds of the air can make nests in its shade." Mark 31:32

Don't underestimate the power of small things. The last few years, while visiting my parents in late summer, I've helped my dad plant turnips in the garden. The turnip seed is amazingly tiny. It's quite remarkable how something so insignificant in size can produce a large root vegetable. For visual consideration, it's a tiny, black speck, similar in size to an unsoaked, dry chia seed or to a grain of iodized salt.

Planting the turnip seed made me think of the size of the mustard seed. It occurred to me that turnips greens are in the same family as mustard greens, so their seeds must be similar in size. I relate to this seed and verse above because it's how I started — with a small seed of faith. Like the farming principles and parables in the Bible, with faithful watering, tending, sowing, weeding, working, waiting, it will grow. It's the same for what a personal, spiritual relationship does within us — it first gets planted within. We water it and tend to it with our habits. Faith grows with us, spiritually moving within, to then move us externally. So, let's get started with step one!

How To Develop Your Spiritual Relationship Step One: Pray

It's easy to underestimate the power of prayer. I mean, it's a simple, small act. It's intangible. How can it make a difference? Well...

Prayer is the #1 step and strategy to get close to your inner voice, ramp up your spiritual relationship, and connect with the Holy Spirit. It's within us. Waiting. We just have to tune in. In my early 40s, as I was looking to deepen my faith, prayer is the one spiritual discipline I started with. In case you haven't prayed before or don't have an active, individual prayer life, I'll share what I've learned about it and steps to either get started or ways to elevate your prayer time. All it takes to uncover the power of prayer, is to do it consistently. And you know what? It's free.

Why Pray?

Recognizing God in our day-to-day life requires knowing God. We get to know God through a solo, dedicated, individual, one-to-one, prayer time. Like any good, strong, trusting relationship, it takes time. We grow our personal connection, our spiritual relationship, with daily, diligent prayer.

Prayer changes our inner view of the outer world. Prayer moves us internally to then be moved externally in new ways.

Prayer is a higher power connection, opening the lines of divine communication. It's direct.

Prayer helps us see into our own heart and to know God's will. It's not always a crystal clear, light bulb moment, but insight is developed and clarity is an outcome with a dedicated, solo prayer practice.

An active prayer life brings spiritual strength. It is powerful. It is a game changer in life. How do I know this? Because it's what started all of this — this being my photography collections, photos of crosses, writing about faith, to then publishing a series of books.

Pray to receive clarity. Ask for direction. What should I do? What does this mean? Use prayer as a strategy to implement a faith-driven life. Whose business plan are you on?

We learn God's leadings steps through prayer. We learn God's voice through prayer. Prayer is a critical step if you want to live a deeper, faith-focused life because it allows you to see God's guiding hand, often in hindsight, but also in valuable daily moments.

Prayer is essential if you wish to step out on faith and follow where God is leading. Why? Because you have to know his voice so you don't get off track and listen to other people's voice, even those well-intentioned. Other people don't know what's in you to do. It hasn't been given to them. It's yours. You have to get close to know and hear. We get close to God in one-to-one prayer.

Prayer gives sustenance. It keeps us spiritually strong. Like doing any exercise or weight training to gain strength and retain muscle tone, it takes consistency to develop, grow, and maintain.

Do you have spiritual strength? Are you aware of the gadget to strengthen our grip? Holding in the hand, the two ends are squeezed together by our fingers and palm. Grip strength is gained only by working the muscles. You work it, to get it. We build strength to hold onto something steady and catch the downward movement of a fall. Spiritual strength does the same. When we encounter a knockout in life, a disappointment, or serious illness that takes us down, how do you pull yourself back up? Prayer keeps us steady and spiritually strong. You have to work it, to get it. What's your grip on prayer?

"Draw near to God and he will draw near to you." James 4:8

How To Pray

What is your opening line? Here's what I've learned about prayer. Keep it simple and focused. People like to overcomplicate things. I've heard acronyms to be used as a prayer guide. I don't remember what they are. I've also heard a prompt that there should be five parts in our prayer time, like the 5 fingers on our hand. I don't remember those either. It makes my head hurt a bit to follow a guide or have five parts to a simple action of prayer. The intent is to be helpful and certainly it works for many people. But overcomplicating a process like can keep people away from doing something simple.

There are two components in a solid prayer. Sometimes all you need is one. As a start, give thanks. That is the difference maker in what is prayer vs. just talking to God. It shows recognition. The second part is to share what's on your mind and ask for direction. That's it.

Below I'm breaking down prayer further to help those who don't currently have an active prayer life and provide helpful tips. Also for those long-time "faith-ers," sharing ways to elevate your prayer life.

Prayer. Part 1: Be thankful.

Here is what I say every day: "Thank you, Lord for waking me up today. Help me do more for you today."

This prayer combines thankfulness and asking. It covers part one and two of a solid prayer. Yes, it's concise. I'm a focused person and not interested in fluff; give me substance.

Sometimes all you need is one part – being thankful. That is enough. It opens your voice to God. Often and throughout the day, just give thanks. "Thank you, Lord for today." It also helps us focus on the present, the now. Not yesterday. Not getting ahead and wondering or worrying about tomorrow. This short prayer helps ground the morning and put us in a place of gratitude.

Start where you feel comfortable. Speak from your heart. Some may prefer a more traditional, formal, written prayer as a guide. If you like that method, find a prayer that resonates with you and gives you the opening stance you enjoy. The Lord's Prayer is a great one and covers all aspects: "Our Father, who art in heaven…" Matthew 6:9-13. It's your prayer time, so you set what works.

"Rejoice always, pray constantly, give thanks in all circumstances;" 1 Thessalonians 5:16-18

Prayer. Part 2: Share what's on your mind and Ask.

This is a combination because they flow together: Share + Ask. When something is on our mind, whether a challenge, a need, a difficulty, or a praise, our ask is directly related to what we share. If I'm down, I share with God that I'm struggling and to help me through this, help me to see the bigger picture.

"Ask and you shall receive." Well, no. Not for anything. Only for what's good for you. Only for what's designed and in the grand plan. We don't always see it at the time, but with prayer and a growing relationship with God, spiritual insight will be developed. Sometimes days, sometimes weeks, sometimes years down the line, we see it and understand.

Prayer works when your prayer is aligned to what God wants for you. When it's aligned to his plan. An example: For years, I was in an up and down intimate relationship. It began with the intent of marriage and seemed so close if we could just get over "this" hump, then it would be smooth. But there was always a hump or hill. I asked God to make it work out. Specifically, my prayer was this: "Lord, help him to see me as his wife." I prayed this solidly for two years. Pretty pathetic really. But I didn't see it at the time. I was so focused on what I wanted. What I thought I needed. What I had spent a lot of time and energy working on. What I thought I loved.

But God didn't let that work out. Two years later, in my second book, *Sights of Faith,* I wrote about learning this angle of prayer, titled My Love, page 3 (the first page): "I'm not going to give what hurts you. Don't you see this? Why do you keep trying, My child? That wish is not my command. You deserve what I give. Your heart is aligned to Me. We are together. You pray for bigger and better things. You've shown I'm the One; the first in your life. My love, I will."

My actual draft of the first line was "I'm not going to give what *keeps* hurting you." I removed "keeps" on review, feeling it opened me up too much. Like everyone would know exactly what I was talking about, a failed intimate relationship. But people don't know. We place far more importance on our own situation than what others can ever realize. I'm sharing it here to illuminate a core principle of prayer. Sure, we can ask for things in prayer, but it has to be aligned to his plans, not ours.

Over the years I've leveled up my prayers, adjusted and developed my own style. You will too. I favor short and concise prayers and then layer them as needed. We pray for the season we're in. The last several years I pray this in my silent, prayer time: "Lord, help me to know. Help me to go." That's it. As I'm writing *Soul Speaking,* I'm also intentional and repeatedly ask the above for my writing. I make progress on the book and then get stuck on how to align the flow or bring it all together. So, I ask: "Lord, help me to know. Help me to go." It's my standard short-hand stance, abbreviated from "Lord, help me to do Your will, help me to glorify You. Help this book be pleasing to You. Help this book to help others find You; bring them closer to You. It is for You. Help me to follow Your direction. You give it to me and I will." These concise and focused prayers reveal a developed, deepened and depended upon spiritual relationship. It's formed from twelve years of consistent, daily, prayer time. We know one another. He knows I will do what he gives me, because I've done it before. Trust is built.

"Rejoice in your hope, be patient in tribulation, be constant in prayer." Romans 12:12

<u>Turnaround Time</u>: Sometimes it's the next day or next week, I have an "ah-ha" moment and see how the random writing parts I want to include fit together and flows. When knowing this new connection, I say aloud: "Thank you, Lord. You are so good! Thank you." It's amazing. Ask. Ask accordingly to his plan. I don't know the master plan, the end point or even what's next year. I keep focused on the right here, right now, being in this season, to write and produce this book.

Let's take a moment to compare. Now, this is quite a different prayer than my earlier example for what I wanted in my narrow, limited view. I was praying for an intimate relationship to work out. "Lord, help him to see me as his wife." Versus: "Lord, help me to do your will and write this book to help others." See the difference? Prayer widens our perspective. Bigger. Better. Bolder.

<u>Answered Prayers</u>: How long does it take? Patience is required. It's not our timeframe. Last year I prayed, "Help me to know. Help me to go," while working in a different direction, doing additional foundational pieces and for more speaking opportunities. But none came. Zero. Zip. Zilch. To say the least, I was disappointed. Maybe it's a not yet. I'm fine with whatever is ahead. Refocusing my efforts, I prayed more and realized this book!

Sometimes hindsight comes many years later. Prayer helps us to know and realize what a season of work, season of pain, or time helping another person was for or why something came in the manner it did.

"Trust in the Lord with all your heart and lean not on your own understanding. In all thy ways acknowledge him, and he shall direct thy paths." Proverbs 3:5-6

Prayer: Optional Part 3: As you deepen your faith, you can add a third element: Apologize.

For an action you've done, should not have taken, or for a situation you could have handled better. In religious terms this is called repent.

Sometimes I pray for how I internally respond to a situation. I may not have externally reacted poorly, as in I wasn't mean. I didn't treat someone negatively as they treated me, but internally I was hot. In those times I pray: "Lord, I'm sorry. I held my tongue, but internally I didn't handle that well. Help me handle that and let it go." I was making a mental list for what I should say, could have said. And maybe what I will say. Know what I mean? The internal dialogue replay that can get looped in your mind? We do need to speak up if there are boundaries crossed or completely unacceptable behavior, but I've learned over the years, I don't need to fight everything. It's not worth my time. Most often, it's a waste of time.

Prayer: Optional Part 4: As you deepen your faith, you can add a fourth element: Pray for others.

People close to you, people who you love, people you value, people who are going through a hard time, like an illness, a job loss, a loss of a loved one, or a challenging time. Pray for your friends to help them continue on their faithful path. Prayer is powerful, not just for your life, but for others as well. God works through people. God blends people in our lives. God loves community. God loves us helping others.

Here's an example: Last year I formed a friendship with a women who is also building a faith-based business. We set up a routine call to share business updates, bounce ideas off each other, get feedback, learn from one another, and support each other. I suggested we add a prayer time to the agenda and asked what I could pray for her about and she did the same for me. Outside of our calls, we each prayed for one another on a daily basis. Then, each meeting we updated each other on our progress for that prayer. It was renewing to have a constant prayer connection with her. I enjoyed praying for her and knowing exactly what to pray in order to help. It was also satisfying to follow-up with each other on a routine basis to hear updates. So often we can pray for someone, but not know the outcome. Additionally, there was an extra bit of comfort in having a continued prayer friend on a deliberate request. We didn't pray during our meeting time. We prayed on our own time for one another.

She also opened my eyes to word choice in prayer. Sharing that she doesn't use the word Father in prayer, (like, "Dear Father, who art in heaven") because she doesn't have a good relationship with hers. Growing up it was a hurtful relationship, so her prayer word choice is different. She also found a hard time connecting in church and didn't attend, but she was very faith-driven woman.

Many times, the main emphasis in prayer groups is on those who are ill, sharing who is in the hospital, and need prayer for healing. Health is important because if we don't have that, it's hard to do anything else in life. But there is more to cover. To dream. Big goals. Big God-given goals. What is it God wants you to do while on this earth? What is your "it?" What's inside you to bring out? Do you know what's on your Heaven-To-Do list? When you get to heaven, will you be able to mark off the items? Pray to know yours.

Other Prayer Considerations:

How long to pray? It doesn't take a set time period. Pray for 30 seconds, 1 minute, 5 minutes, 10 or 15 minutes. Start. However it flows, don't be concerned with how long. When your heart is in the right place, God knows. Anytime is the right time to pray. When you wake up, while driving to work, in the shower, making a meal, taking a walk, or in a certain chair or prayer nook you may designate. Pray any and everywhere.

<u>Solo prayer</u>: This is just you. It's individual. Not with your spouse, partner, small group, or another believer. Those are all great prayer times, but it's not a replacement for your own, 1:1 prayer time. Solo prayer time stacks. Solo time goes deeper. In group prayer you are set to the facilitator's time. Solo prayer you are set to your spirit time. You can go longer. You get closer to your inner spirit and form a deeper connection to the Holy Spirit, allowing you to hear. If you attend church, praying in service as a group together, isn't the same as praying yourself. There is additional power of prayer done in private (Matthew 6:6).

<u>Words to use</u>: There is a reverence in prayer, to come in a respectful manner and recognize the time as divine. It is holy. How do you refer to God? I use Lord and God in my prayers. "Lord, help me to..." Other reverential words for the person you are speaking to are: Jesus, Lord Jesus, Christ, Father, and/or Heavenly Father. For those that may be newer to faith and not have a defined connection to God, you could use Heavenly Creator, Divine Creator, or Holy Spirit. Use what fits for you.

The important aspect is recognition of a higher, bigger power. A divine power. There is holy reverence in knowing there is God, even if you haven't personally felt it yet. Or if you have felt spiritual, but haven't known how to link it further, prayer helps lead the way to make the connection. Don't get hung up on what word(s) to use. Just start. God knows your heart.

Note: You don't have to be "religious" in order to believe, or have a relationship with God, and to pray. Religion is a formal, traditional practice with buildings and a church of people. God isn't contained to buildings. We don't have to go to church to have a spiritual relationship and holy connection. He is bigger than a place and is an ultimate Divine Connector. Always waiting and at your ready. There's never a busy signal. You are not placed on hold or have to go through multiple phone prompts to leave a message. You have direct contact. It starts with your internal voice and spirit. That's the cool thing about prayer and God, it just takes starting. Any time. Any day. Any place.

It's your time: It's not about being eloquent or using an abundance of big, flowing words. Be humble. Your words, your heart, your time.

Be bold with your prayers: You many have heard the saying "Let the size of your goal be the size of your God." What are you praying for? God can do more than just bless this food to the nourishment of our bodies.

How often to pray? Daily. Multiple times throughout the day. You get out of it, what you put into it. Just like physical exercise and strength training for the body or education for our mind, prayer is gaining spiritual strength. It's our spiritual health. Spirit to mind to body.

Faith Nugget: You can believe in God, but not know him. Those who know each other, call one another by name. Close relationships have regular communication. We don't get close without putting in the 1:1 time in prayer. Does God know your voice? He knows it when you pray. When he hears from you directly. Do you know his voice? You learn it in solo prayer, to feel it and know it.

"When you pray, I will listen." Jeremiah 29:12

Ways to Level-up Your Prayer:

Want spiritual purpose in life? Want an edge in life? Pray. Be ready.

Because we only get deeper spiritual insight when we are open and listen to that voice, the inner knowing, and act. To follow where God is leading. Prayer opens the way.

Key point: Developing your spiritual relationship with prayer is not a one-time event or once in a while. It's not a one-way street. It's a relationship. To get more from it, we have to be open. This means listening. To hear. This is a give and take. You give your time. You give your heart. You receive what God gives you. You take his words. You take his leading. This is a process to learn and to do.

It's a leveling up, continuing process. Progress is a natural by-product of prayer. Your heart changes with prayer. Your heart opens with prayer. More is involved. You want to do more because it fills you. It fills the holes you have inside; your cup runneth over. Overflowing. It quenches the thirst and brings up more within your spiritual well. John 4:13, "whoever drinks of the water that I shall give him will never be thirsty." Isaiah 55:1, NIV, "Come, all you who are thirsty, come to the waters." Our spiritual relationship is what quenches our worldly thirst.

Sharing what I've learned about how to level-up the spiritual discipline of prayer.

Level Up: Pray Three Little Words

Want a real leveling up in life? Pray these 3 words.

"God, use me." Caveat: These 3 words are not for the faint of heart.

That's what I did. For 18 months I prayed "God, use me." Nothing happened externally, but internally, I was growing a personal relationship with God. Then when I did have a spiritual knowing, I took action on the first idea. Concerted, consistent steps of faith.

It's continued for ten years. These 3 words can transform your life. I know because it did for me.

It's an unassuming, simple and straight-forward approach. Pray and you will receive. Seek and you shall find. God knows your heart. God likes to grow things, to grow within our heart — to plant and grow ideas within us. It starts with our internal, personal spiritual relationship, connection with our spirit and to the Holy Spirit.

Because Why Else Would I Do This?

Faith is not my background. It's not my formal education or professional chosen career. I never wanted to write or be an author. Photography wasn't an interest or hobby of mine; never took classes.

The point being, prayer opens our heart. Our eyes see anew when our heart opens and is led by the Spirit, when we let faith take hold. There is a direct connection to our heart and our eyes. In-sight. My eyes began seeing crosses all around me when I deepened my personal relationship and prayed.

"Give me your heart, and let your eyes observe my ways."
Proverbs 23:26

Level Up: Pray in the Closet

Yes, literally, your closet. It's simple. Go into your closet, sit on the floor and shut the door. If needed for comfort, use a chair. I use my bedroom closet and sit on the floor. Any closet will work, a small space with a door. Try it.

This is a leveling up prayer time. Why? It provides the immediate stillness to couple with the practice. Nothing to distract and nothing else to focus on in the enclosed space. Sometimes complete darkness or a sliver of light from the narrow opening at the bottom of the door, I can barely see my feet and toes. Sitting cross-legged on the floor, the only space needed and had.

In the closet, I spend more time in prayer. As noted previously, I don't have long prayers, I'm concise and repeat short prayers throughout the day. However, when I go into my closet and pray, I'll spend 10-15 minutes, sometimes more.

Visualize you in your closet it: It's dark. A place removed from activity and possible disruption. A specific space set aside. It's silent. Focused. Intentional. Nothing glamorous. It's a space to get closer. Consider it in your prayer practice. Once you start, you'll probably continue it. Why? Because it has a feel. Your spirit knows it.

"But when you pray, go into your room and shut the door and pray to your Father who is in secret; and your Father who sees in secret will reward you." Matthew 6:6

From the King James Version "when thou prayest, enter into thy *closet*." Matthew 6:6

Praying in the closet didn't naturally come to me. I received it from my cousin. During a long hike, talking about faith, she mentioned praying in her closet. Really? Eight years later, I implemented it. A nugget that stuck, my curiosity piqued, because I never heard it before. Being a new concept, I remember visualizing it, her going into her bedroom closet. This visual seed was planted and took hold in my mind. An additional key point here is how sharing our faith, even small details, the technical aspects of how we practice faith, helps others to build their own. What may seem mundane to some, can be powerful faith nuggets for others to apply in life.

Level Up: Spiritual Fast with Prayer

Another leveling up is to pair a spiritual fast coupled with focused prayer. Why? A reduction of food brings a heightened focus on our spiritual knowing. Fasting reduces the noise of the world. It allows our soul senses to become closer; attuned with the Holy Spirit. It's divine guidance, it's receiving an understanding of the bigger picture. It's a holy strategy session to hear and receive more; to know the next steps God wants us to take.

The Bible routinely includes the coupling of these two actions, "with prayer and fasting." But how often do we really take the extra step to fast? It's not enjoyable. We like to eat. It's not hard though, but it does take discipline and is known as a spiritual discipline many Christians complete annually.

Last year I did a spiritual fast (my second one; the first I did 6 years prior). Why did I do it? It gets to the heart. In early January, I prayed for God to help me know the next step and for clarity with a book. I prayed that if I'm meant to write another book, to let me know it. Asking for knowledge and wisdom is leveled up prayer.

Outcome: The last day of my fast, day six, this book came to me. Literally, light bulb on! "I see it! Yes, God." I didn't know this was in me, but I had these photos that spoke to my soul over four years with no plans to do anything with them. After the spiritual fast I realized a greater theme linking these photos together and how a book could flow. I had clarity for the bigger message. I immediately started working on it and as I did so, the book grew and expanded. Initially, I tried to contain it and keep it in one book. But there was more than one could hold. I had to do two books. *Soul Speaking* is the first; stay tuned for the next book. It all came to me through the combination of prayer and fasting. Takeaway: It's worth doing a focused spiritual fast annually. Have you done one?

How To Develop Your Spiritual Relationship Step Two: Be Still

Stillness is quiet time by yourself. Stillness is an absence of noise. It's focused time to be alone and get connected with your spirit, to hear your inner voice.

Stillness is taking time to receive. It's time to be. It's being, not doing. Being where you can hear your soul speaking. It's focused time away from noise and disruption. This can be achieved in a space you feel comfortable and connected to. Be it in nature, in a chair, or in the closet. It doesn't need to be any particular place. Just anywhere in your home.

Stillness is enjoying the absence of activity. It's silence. Ahhhh. It's soothing to our soul.

Why Be Still?

Stillness prepares us to know God's voice. Stillness allows us to tune into our senses. Stillness deepens our spiritual relationship and is required for spiritual insight. It's being by yourself in order to hear your soul speaking.

"Be still, and know that I am God. I am exalted among the nations; I am exalted in the earth!" Psalm 46:10

In order to be still, we have to remove ourselves from "noise clutter," making time for our spiritual health. Why?

If we always have noise and activity around us, it's very hard to connect and hear our spirit and the Holy Spirit doesn't compete for it. Make the time or you lose out. The Holy Spirit, God words in subtle ways. It's quiet. We have to be still to know it. "Be still and know." Stillness comes before knowing. Time in silence is how we can hear our soul speak. What bubbles up from within? Make notes. Pay attention to repeating patterns.

Noise is a distraction: Some of it is toxic, highway noise, construction, sirens, city noise, traffic, dogs barking, etc. Those are external noises, let alone how many people keep constant noise around them by listening to music, talking on the phone, listening to podcasts, or having the TV on in the background. A constant plugged-in state of sound going into our ears and body. Some live in a constant state of noise. If you are used to that level of sound (noise), it could be unsettling for you to consider silence. If this is you, it's why you need it. Your spirit, your inner world, your nervous system, needs a break.

Stillness is a space within us. Our spirit is a sensory mechanism. We humans like to overestimate our ability to multitask, but studies show it doesn't lead to greater productivity or mental gains when we switch between multiple projects and thought processes, because we have to re-engage when switching from one task to another. Or we all know how being on our phone for emailing over a meal while trying to have a conversation with another person doesn't work. It's incomplete flow of sharing. Our senses (sight, sound, perception, stimuli) can't focus on multiple, competing elements. It's too much. It's the same with our spirit.

Our eyes and senses don't multi-task. Anyone else turn off the music in the car to parallel park, or with important directions to make sure not to miss the turnoff. It's in this same flow, imagine what you miss when constantly caught in "noise-clutter." Whether it is external noise you can't escape or the direct noise you can control like listening to music, audio books or a podcast while taking a walk. You will miss out on noticing things around you. You will miss out on what you could be thinking about, what your spirit can attune to. What your senses notice, see and feel.

Noise is a silencer to our inner voice. It holds in what your inner spirit yearns to bring up, via your thoughts, thinking, and ideas.

If you are resistant to time in stillness, you need it. Your mind is overruling what your innate soul needs for nourishment. Don't feel it? Develop it. Our spirit is naturally soothing. The Spirit is good.

Refocus with Stillness
From the mind of doing to the spirit of being:

Mind: Rushed   Spirit: Soothed
Mind: Preoccupied   Spirit: Present
Mind: Distracted   Spirit: Filled
Mind: Adding to your schedule   Spirit: Open
Mind: Reactive   Spirit: Response/Choice
Mind: Busy   Spirit: Free
Mind: Anxious   Spirit: Calm

Implementing Stillness

To be versus to go. Being vs. doing. People who have a hard time not "going," not being "busy," not being "productive" with a quantifiable measure of output for a unit of time, please note, this could feel challenging and uncomfortable. Reducing the busy thoughts, the never ending "to-do" lists, to calm the anxious mind, and to not be productive is the lack of calm spirit. Our spirit needs self-care. It's okay to not account for each and every hour. There is no permission slip needed to slow down, to be still and be. It's your own stamp of self-care. It's for you. It's for your soul. It's to help hear your spirit and connect with the Holy Spirit.

For those who may have anxiety, or are more anxious in general, this can be challenging. It's why you should incorporate stillness and not avoid it. Practical guidance: As an introductory step to stillness, while doing household activities don't have background noise on. No TV. No streaming shows. No music. No talking on the phone. Just carry on and do the dishes, clean, laundry in silence. It's quiet. Can you hear yourself, your inner voice? Give it time.

Take a walk or sit outside without noise. Don't call someone to pass the time. No music playlist. No podcast. No audio book. No book to read. Just be. What will your mind and spirit share with you? Next phase: Sit and be still. Start small— 5 min in silence. Absorb it. Practice deep breathing with longer exhales if you have a hard time.

In time of stillness, pay attention to what you think about. What raises up from within? This is your spirit, your inner voice, your soul. To remember, make notes for what raises up so over time you can find patterns. What is repeating?

Ways to Level Up Stillness

Go deeper and spend time in solitude. What is this? It's a lot more stillness and quiet. It's a focused reduction and elimination of noise. It's choosing to spend time away from social events, removing yourself from social interactions. It helps to tune even further into our spirit and connection to God. Think monk-like, but not as drastic. Spend some weekends "in" — not going out, not being with others, not being seen, not doing activities with friends, not being entertained by others or needing other's company.

Solitude is a focus on our inner being. Knowing our inner self. It's alone time, but it's not lonely. It's rejuvenating.

Stillness Takeaways:

- If you always have surrounding noise and activity, you miss out hearing your spirit. The Holy Spirit doesn't compete for your attention.
- "Be still and know." Key point: Stillness precedes knowing.
- Stillness is taking time to receive. It's time to be, not do.

How To Develop Your Spiritual Relationship. Step Three: Be Grateful

Develop a spirit of gratitude. Gratitude makes a space in your heart for more love. It's God's pathways to your soul.

A spirit of gratitude gives off an inner glow. It's a light within. No one can take it. It's your joy.

Gratitude gives grace. For yourself and to others. It opens your heart to love; you rise above. That's not to say you accept bad behavior, it's removing yourself from needing to fight it. You step aside. You let it roll by instead of engaging with it— the other person and their own fears, lack of. Refer to "Letting Go To Move Forward."

Your internal spiritual relationship is an inner flame. When you feed it, it burns. Like those orange coals in a hot fire, it's ignited. How does your spirit burn? Is it trying to catch hold of the flick? Are you giving it air? Our ideas are a spark to start the fire and feeding the flame is an ongoing process with implementation. Are you breathing life into your daily spiritual disciplines?

Our inner fire won't grow without our individual effort. Like a wood fireplace, it doesn't burn without added logs and attention to stoke and shift the wood. Coals stay hot for a while, but grow cold with no attention. Is your internal, personal, spiritual relationship cold? Or hot? What actions do you take to bring it alive, to keep it burning?

Why Gratitude?

Gratitude changes our focus. It's not what other people are doing to us. It's not taking things personally. It's not what someone didn't do when we thought they should do XYZ. Those are all external circumstances. Gratitude changes our internal view so we can see the external world differently. Simple. It's strategic.

Change Your View and the View Changes

Here's an example, I used to live near the Nelson-Atkins Museum of Art in Kansas City. On my morning walks I often took photos of the iconic, giant Shuttlecock sculptures placed on the outdoor lawn. Then one day, I stood under one of them (the one on the north lawn is slightly tilted to accommodate). I took a photo standing under it, looking up, through the orange tipped base. "Well, isn't that an interesting view." It was so different from all my other photos and provided a unique perspective of the clouds through a small framed opening. The inside was quite spacious and I noticed the fine ribbed detailing on the white feather-top section of the sculpture. I didn't know these points when standing from a distance. That's what gratitude does. It shifts our focus and helps us see from a new angle.

These large-scale Shuttlecock sculptures show that even small, insignificant objects can be something grand by changing their size. A shuttlecock is from the game of badminton. For a reference point or to see the sculpture, turn to the last page of this book. One of the Claes Oldenburg and Coosje van Bruggen Shuttlecocks made the cover of *In Plain Sight Volume II* with a shadow of an Everyday Cross landing just right, in the shaded grass.

This is what gratitude does, it changes the scale of how we see things, through growing our spiritual discipline. It helps to transform ordinary aspects of life into something extraordinary. Gratitude helps us see a bigger picture.

Gratitude is spiritual renewal. It changes how we view external happenings, starting on the inside. Gratitude opens the internal eyes of our spirit so we can see what's important. In-sight. It awakens our soul to connect to the Holy Spirit.

"having the eyes of your hearts enlightened, that you may know what is the hope to which he has called you, what are the riches of his glorious inheritance in the saints," Ephesians 1:18

Gratitude Changes Our Heart

Gratitude helps to see the good, when times are bad. When life is hard, illness, unexpected loss of a person or a job, a broken relationship, or challenging children. When what you expected doesn't turn out, when you aren't where you thought you'd be, focus on gratitude.

Gratitude gives us space to see all the things that are good in our life, especially when the front-and-center problem are overtly large scale and apparent. When we take time to notice and give thanks for minor, small things, being appreciative of all the things that are going good, and not a focus on what isn't happening, our heart grows closer to God. Gratitude opens our heart to receive more.

Often people want the big things in life and miss the joy of small delights. Always looking for epic, grand, big, you can miss the finer points of God's details. Gratitude gives us space in our heart to find joy in small things. Gratitude helps us see luxuries we take for granted. Big and small. Deep and wide.

A Divine Connection Point: Nature

Appreciation for small things shifts our attention to recognize meaning and a higher power. That's where spending time in nature helps us observe all the wonderful details, little joys and cultivate a spirit of gratitude. Time outdoors rejuvenates us in natural ways that can not be replicated in artificial environments and time indoors. Numerous studies solidify the health benefits of nature to include reducing stress when hearing birdsong, improved concentration and decreased mental fatigue when walking in green spaces vs. urban concrete zones. By design, nature is an opening for gratitude, restoring our spirit. God created it. Mother Nature is a worship zone.

"Am I not everywhere in all heaven and earth?" Jeremiah 23:24

Ways to Level Up Gratitude

<u>Not complaining</u>: Not griping about situations that occur or are annoying. Sure, yes, there are frustrations and things to share with others, but keep it in check. Continuous complaining is not a joyful spirit; it is the opposite of gratitude. Move your heart and spirit to move your mind out of this hardening. Consider your words. How do you speak? What words do you use? Words flow from our heart.

Gratitude transforms our inner voice, our thoughts, our heart, for it to then be reflected on the outer. What we speak. What we say. Projection, our voice, is what we think within. Our words are not random. Our words are intentional, planted within our heart and spirit from what we feed it. Good seeds can turn bad based on the water and nutrients provided and our environment — the people we choose to be around and to stay around. People are an influence. Choose wisely. What do you cultivate?

"For out of the abundance of the heart the mouth speaks."
Matthew 12:34

Not being negative: Not going with the flow of negative conversation or gossip of those around you. Not talking about or pointing out the bad things, but to see the good. Be the good. It takes spiritual strength to shift our mindset from negative to positive. If something keeps happening to you, what is your contribution to the situation?

Resetting a negative situation: What comes our way in life? Most all of the time we have a choice how to respond. Ideally, it is to respond purposefully and to not react out of our emotions. We can still be frustrated, but there's no need to share it with the other party. It's a distraction. Handle the circumstance and move on. When we keep talking about it, sharing it with others, its kept alive, feeding into negative energy. Move swiftly to neutralize it. Receive the occurrence as an opportunity to learn. Ask yourself: What is this teaching me? What can I learn about myself in this situation? What led to this? How can I handle this better next time?

Developing a spirit of gratitude gives our mind the ability to reset and recover quicker from negative situations — to see through a lens of faith. From spirit to mind into action.

"Keep your heart with all vigilance; for from it flow the springs of life." Proverbs 4:23

Gratitude Takeaways:

- Gratitude makes a space in our heart for more love. It's God's pathway to our soul.

- Gratitude changes our focus. It changes our internal view so we can see the external world differently. Change your view and the view changes.

- Gratitude opens our heart. Gratitude opens the way to see. From our heart and spirit to our eyes.

Progress is a stacking process.
A small, daily Bible reading habit, naturally grows within us —
in our spirit. The Word gets into our heart.

How To Develop Your Spiritual Relationship
Step Four: Read the Bible

Reading the Bible provides a blueprint and connects us with the Holy Spirit. Reading the Bible daily goes deeper, soaking into us. Here's why.

The thing about reading the Bible daily is it gets into our heart. And when we develop and deepen a personal, spiritual relationship with God, the heart leads in life. Well, that is if we choose to listen, yes? The mind likes to overrule. That is why we need a daily habit of it, to rewire the brain to God, not us. We need a daily habit of it to develop our spiritual health, to bring the most out of our spirit.

It doesn't take a large time commitment. Some days my Bible reading is 5 minutes. Some days it's 20 minutes if I go deeper and look up different translations or make notes.

Photo Left: The four Bibles I've read, cover-to-cover. Top of the stack is The Revised Standard Version-1952, my father's Bible, most recently finished.

Here is a practical guide for how to implement a Bible reading practice and why this spiritual discipline is so important.

Make a Place for Bible Reading

I read at the same place, spot every day. I call it my nook. It's at the end of my couch. The Bible has the spotlight. There is also a lamp on the end table and a fabric coaster for my coffee. That's it. Why? The Bible is the focus. It's the priority. I like seeing it there throughout the day. I don't move it to a bookshelf or place in a drawer to pull out the next morning. Prominence. Place. Priority.

Dedicate a Time to Read Your Bible

I have the same time every day for my bible reading. It's when I wake. It's not at a specific time, like 5:15 a.m., but it follows a set routine. It flows. This type of discipline helps keep the habit. Every day. How long I have done this? At the time of this book publishing, 9.5 years.

I do mornings because of the first fruits principle to give my first portion to God. My best portion is morning. It's when I have my best energy and my mind is at its peak, so I give it to God. I want him in my beginning thoughts to guide the day. As opposed to the end of the day, in bed, when I'm tired, ready to rest and could fall asleep. If your energy is best at night, then this time could work for you. But waiting until the end of the day makes it easy to drop the habit, or skip a day, when unplanned events occur. Just like exercise, it's easy to make excuses or get distracted when the day takes over and it's left to the last hours.

Make a commitment to the time that works for you and stick to it. One year I had consulting project with a global client working with groups in Italy, France, Spain and other countries. Most days I had meetings begin at 5:00 a.m. CST time. Because I was leading the project and the meetings, not just being a participant, I had to be ready and prepared in advance of 5 a.m. I set my alarm for 3:30 to wake early for my Bible reading and quiet morning time. Did I really want to get up that early? No. But I couldn't wait until later in the day for it. I value Bible time being first. I won't push it off. I'm sharing this as an example of sticking to the commitment. Once you make excuses for skipping a day, it's a downhill slide. There are differences for a reason and an excuse. Many people don't see their own excuses and label it a reason. When you have a choice, own it.

"And in the morning, a great while before day, he rose and went out to a lonely place, and there he prayed." Mark 1:35

Plan How to Read the Bible

Some prefer to follow a guided Bible reading plan, like "Read the Bible in One Year." It's good if you want a formal structure. Not me. Don't rush me. I'm not on a preset timeline. I'm following my spirit.

The first Bible I read I spent more time in it because it was a study bible, extra thick with long footnotes and I read every bit of the tissue thin pages. As I developed this spiritual discipline, I landed on reading 1-2 chapters every day. In these short sessions, I can grasp the meaning and go deeper on each bit. It grants time to think and absorb.

My viewpoint on an optimal pace for reading the Bible is this: Slow is smooth and smooth is fast. It's not a race. The goal is not speed. It's depth. Like a nice, easy, soaking rainfall compared to a downpour thunderstorm. The slow rain brings nourishing refreshment, going deep into the roots. The later rapid rush of rainfall brings volumes that has run-off; not all of the water is able to be contained (caught). Water can cause flooding. It can be too much, too fast where it can't be absorbed as well as a slow trickle. That's how I view Bible reading. Let it soak into your spirit. It goes deeper when it's slow and steady.

Some people have a set time for how long they will read each day. Do what you feel your spirit needs. Adjust it as needed until you find your natural rhythm.

Key: Creating a simple structure increases your chances to make the habit of Bible reading stick.

Natural Influences: Backstory

I received the idea to continue reading the Bible cover-to-cover from my grandmother, my mom's mother, when visiting her on the farm.

She didn't go to church. She didn't express or talk about faith other than telling me she prayed for me every day. I didn't know her as a woman of faith. But on this visit, her Bible was out and open on the kitchen table. I asked about it and learned it was her seventh time reading it. Asking what she liked about reading it, she said, "Oh, it has some really good stories."

Reading different Bible versions naturally flowed after I read my first one because I then wanted to read the Bible that Jean, a dear friend who I lovingly refer to as my adopted grandmother, had given me. It was a King James Version. After reading that one, I pulled out my Bible from confirmation days, it was New International Version and I read it. After that one I asked my parents if they had other versions and then read from my father's Bible, a Revised Standard Version-1952 edition.

Still today, when reading the Bible, ten years later, I've thought: "Grandma, you're right. There are some really good stories." There's wisdom in what we can pick up from our elders. It's not always what is spoken that carries the most influence, it's what is shown in action, what we observe. Plus, God uses people to show us the way. My grandmother never said I should read the Bible nor did she ask if I had read it. She didn't need to. The seed was planted.

For How Long?

Always. Once I started, I couldn't stop. Try it out yourself. I'll continue this practice of reading my Bible daily for all my days ahead. My grandmother was 88 and on her seventh time reading the Bible. In ten years (9.5 to be exact) I've read it four times, a different Bible version each time. I'm in no rush. There is no competition. I have no grand plan for how many times my lifetime will hold. The important part is the practice. I hope this encourages you to start a Bible reading practice.

Why Make a Daily Habit of Bible Reading?

You may think you don't need to. But here are some reasons I've learned why it's a deeply rewarding and valuable discipline in life. Reading daily, it gets in you. Soaking *into*. The Bible is the original motivational speaker to move us. First within, internally, in spirit and then externally, into action. Spirit to mind to body.

If you want more meaning and spiritual purpose in life, it's a prerequisite. If you want spiritual insight and to know God's will for your life, reading the Bible is a requirement. How important is spiritual insight to you? To have discernment? To understand God's leading hand in your life? Want spiritual clarity? Then you do all 5 Steps to Develop Your Spiritual Relationship to get close, including daily Bible reading. If serious, you will.

Heart

We know God by knowing His heart. What he treasures. We learn this by knowing his Book, His words.

The "Living Word" of the Bible brings a holy beat to our heart – a direct line to our spirit, connecting with the Holy Spirit. It's a divine connection. From our spirit it then renews our mind. Our mind then directs our thoughts, our steps, and our actions. Did you catch that order of significance? Spirit, mind, body. That is the healthy holy order. Spirit is first. Not the worldly, wellbeing framework of mind, body, spirit.

Yes, you can still have faith and be faithful and not read the Bible daily. Certainly. But I know this at a personal level. I have only been able to grow my faith at deeper levels and have the courage to continue stepping out on faith, because I read it daily (along with prayer and the other steps). As I actively took steps of faith, I related to the Bible. Reading it, doing it, being it. It goes hand in hand. Hands. Our hands working it. Our hands holding a Bible. I still like the real thing of a tangible book. It brings me closer. It holds me.

"The beginning of wisdom is this: Get wisdom, and whatever you get, get insight." Proverbs 4:7

How Often to Read the Bible?

Daily. Not just Sunday. Daily gets into you. Daily it grows. Daily it is alive. It is our daily nutrient. Our soul, our spirit, needs daily feeding.

Have you heard the Bible referred to as the "Living Word?" I never understood this until I practiced it daily. The Word is alive. There's an energy when it touches you. There's divine timing when the exact day, the words you read are what you needed — the Scripture and meaning fit. It hits. It lights you up, giving your spirit a spark of life.

"Give us this day our daily bread." Matthew 6:11

How I Read the Bible

<u>How much</u>? I read one or two chapters every morning. It's easily doable for anyone. It's *only* 1-2 chapters. It just takes discipline. Develop a routine to make it simple. Simple things stick.

<u>Real paper or digital Bible</u>? It's personal preference. For me, holding a physical Bible brings a closeness into the spiritual relationship, making it tangible. To be in reach. I'm a tactile person and like to touch things, so for me it's a paper Bible I can feel. I like the weight of it. And when faith and spiritual connection can be an intangible form of measure, the holding of a real Bible can give connection.

Intention for Bible reading: Over the years I've developed saying this phrase at the start: "Lord, help me to love you, serve you and know you." I use this same phrasing every day as a way to bring focus and intent to the time. It's grounding and sets the tone for the day ahead. I look forward to the daily time. This year as I walk to my Bible nook, I found myself saying "What do you have for me today, Lord?"

Bible reading tip: I use a bookmark, but with small print, there can be 4-5 chapters over two pages when opening the Bible. I often don't recall where I stopped the day prior. To help, after reading, I place a dot at the end of the chapter finished as a marker for my starting point the next day. A small dot provides the exact point. Again, make it easy. I use a Micron 005 archival ink, very fine tip marker in blue. I also use this to underline and date verses that resonate or to write a few words, a short note, in the margin. Some people use color highlighters in their Bible. Not me. It's distracting to my eyes; I prefer simplicity. Do what works best and helps you.

Ways to Level Up Your Bible Time

Read the Bible in a different version. Go deeper in your Bible reading practice: when a verse jumps out to you, compare other Bible versions, like the King James Version or the New Living, etc.

Words have meaning, matter and are important for our understanding. Words convey intent and sometimes versions offer a slightly different meaning or opening into a new thought. If you are a "word person," you'll enjoy it. To compare verses that resonate with you, use the YouVersion Holy Bible app, it's free. Reading a different Bible translation than the one you're most accustomed to can bring new insight and connection. Even slight subtleties can increase understanding. When we know the significance and meaning, we learn and can apply it.

The Bible was written from a different time of living, which brings different word utilizations, concepts, and interpretation. Word meanings can shift over time. Additionally, The Old Testament was written in Latin; The New Testament in Hebrew. This brings complexity of understanding original intent and word origin.

Here is an example of a difference that jumped out to me. Reading in the Revised Standard Version-1952, the word "revive" was used instead of the word "refresh." Compare below:

"The law of the Lord is perfect, *reviving* the soul; the testimony of the Lord is sure, making wise the simple;" Psalm 19:7

"The law of the Lord is perfect, *refreshing* the soul. The statutes of the Lord are trustworthy, making wise the simple." Psalm 19:7 NIV

"Revive" has a stronger and deeper meaning. To bring to life, there is movement, it connects to breath and is an action of transformation. Whereas the word "refresh" is helpful and renewing, something to bring relief. "Revive" is life. It's more powerful. What do you think?

Bible Reading Takeaways:

• There's power in small, consistent, daily habits. It doesn't matter how long it takes or that you finish a Bible reading plan in one year. God knows our heart. Do you know his?

• Key points: Creating a simple structure increases your chances to make the habit of Bible reading stick. Discipline is just a routine.
1) Make a place to read your Bible. 2) Set a general time/timeframe. 3) Decide how you will read: follow a guided reading plan, read x number of chapters/day, or for a set amount of time.

How To Develop Your Spiritual Relationship
Step Five: Memorize Scripture

To memorize something is to know it by heart. Memorizing requires more. It's with this process that memorizing Bible verses brings the message closer to our heart. Within us. Into. No external reference point needed. Heart and spirit: this is a unifying connection. From the heart/spirit, it flows into our mind.

Why Memorize Scripture?

We memorize Bible verses because they are God's message. It's how we can know him better. To know his words within. Deeper. Reciting memorized Scripture is a love language.

Heart

It shows who we love. It shows a priority. It's important enough to memorize. It's easy to be familiar with many verses, but what do you hold close to your heart? What do you value enough to commit it to memory? To set above? To prioritize?

Here's why it's so powerful. It's in you. Within. Close. Simple, right? You know it. Scripture goes deeper when we know it by heart. When we pull upon the words, bring them up, and recite them aloud or inwardly with ourself. Meditate on them, which is just repeating the full verse many times in a row. There is reverence in memorizing Bible verses.

<u>Definition: Revere</u> (verb): To show devoted deferential honor to. Synonyms include worship, adore, venerate. Venerate, in definition, implies a holding as holy.

Repeating Bible verses gains deeper understanding. Focus on different parts of the verse and words as you recite and repeat. Memorizing Scripture comforts. It's calming. It increases our connection and closeness to God. It's a direct line.

You might be thinking, "Hey, I can easily do a quick internet search and read verses." But you're missing the point. That is not the same. You can also refer to verses saved in notes or a Bible app easily, but that too is not the same. It's like before we all had cell phones. Remember what we had? Landlines. And we called phone numbers. We actually knew phone numbers because we dialed them, going through the motion, one number by one number. Going through the process, we often memorized them. Still today, I know my best friend's home number by heart and my parent's home number, even though they are no longer used by them. However, a number I call often with my cell phone, I don't know. None are stored in me. We call cell numbers all the time, yet we don't know the number. It's a similar analogy with Scripture. It takes more to store it within us. Deeper. Memorize verses to know it.

When we go through hard times in life, memorizing Bible verses provides coverage. It's like a blanket we can cuddle up with. Because it's so close, the divine words held within, it's especially comforting when we find ourselves in a deeper need, an unexpected low.

For When You Cry in The Shower

Memorized Scripture is helpful for when you cry. It's helpful to have something within you, in your heart, in your mind, in your spirit to help turn your thoughts around and keep you focused on God, for hope and calm. One of my favorites for uplift is "Create a clean heart in me, O God, and renew a steadfast spirit within me." Psalm 51:10

It's right there for us to pull upon. It's an instant salve to our soul. During a hard time in life, there were a few years I found myself crying in the shower. It's not a time to turn to your phone for a verse saved. It's amazing how just a handful of memorized verses stored within can revive a weary spirit. It's strategic spiritual coverage. Memorizing Scripture grows our faith, moving us into a space of spiritual strength. It keeps the message alive within us.

Now, let's review how to memorize scripture. Here's what I did to learn verses.

How to Memorize Scripture in 3 Steps:

<u>1. Pick a verse you connect with.</u>
Select something that catches your attention or relates to what's happening in your life. It's easier to remember and memorize a verse you relate to —it will stick with you.

<u>2. Use visual cues to help you remember.</u>
As an example: The first verse I memorized is 1 Peter 5:6-7: "Humble yourselves, therefore, under God's mighty hand, he will lift you up in due time. Cast all your anxieties on him because he cares for you."
For the first part of the verse, the cues I used were to see myself in a kneeling pose for the "humble yourself." I visualized a gigantic hand for "God's mighty hand." Then for the "he will lift you up" I thought of puppets on strings, marionettes, being raised. The second sentence of "cast your anxieties on him because he cares" flowed because I was going through a hard time and connected with this statement so it was easier to recall.

<u>3. Practice reciting.</u>
We learn it by saying it repeatedly. Combine this practice time into what you already do and be strategic to utilize downtimes. Recite while getting ready for the day, when driving, idle time in the car or waiting in lines, or while taking a walk (instead of listening to music or podcasts). Keep the verse in your phone or on a written pad of paper to reference and double check as you practice.

Memorizing Scripture develops our spiritual relationship and grows us closer with God.

Consideration Points: Memorize verses that resonate with you. I have a core set of around ten verses I recite the most. Another five or so I have memorized, but don't use as often. It's not exhaustive. It doesn't need to be. It's not a requisite we memorize 50 or 100 verses. It's quality over quantity. God knows our heart. We memorize Scripture to know his. Start simple and build. The first year I memorized 4 verses and kept a log. The following year I added another 4. Today, ten years in, I still use that same list, kept in my phone Notes, titled "Memorized Scripture." Novel naming convention! Keep it simple.

Memorize the Book, Chapter & Verse: Retain all the key aspects so you can reference it or share with someone. Reference points matter. Example: Jeremiah 29:13. Sometimes it's harder to remember the chapter and verse number. I stretch myself to do so. Do what you can. The important part is memorizing the words to get into your heart and spirit.

While taking a walk: A verse to consider is "Keep steady my steps according to thy promise, and let no iniquity get dominion over me." Psalms 119:133. I added this two years ago because it jumped out to me while reading the Bible. It resonates with me as I continue to step out on faith and I also enjoy walking. I also use this verse in my prayer closet time.

If you are new to memorizing Scripture, to help get started, here are the ones I began with and are core verses I still hold close.

1. "Humble yourselves, therefore, under God's mighty hand, that he will lift you up in due time. Cast all your anxiety on him because he cares for you." 1 Peter 5:6-7 NIV

2. "Create in me a clean heart, O God, and renew a steadfast spirit within me." Psalm 51:10 NIV

3. "Trust in the Lord with all your heart and lean not on your own understanding; in all your ways submit to him, and he will make your paths straight." Proverbs 3:5-6 NIV

4. "Let the morning bring me word of your unfailing love, for I have put my trust in you. Show me the way I should go, for to you I entrust my life." Psalm 143:8 NIV

5. "Be joyful in hope, patient in affliction, and faithful in prayer." Romans 12:12 NIV

6. "Let us run with endurance the race that lies before us, keeping our eyes on Jesus, the source and perfecter of our faith." Hebrews 12:1-2 NIV

7. "You will seek me and find me; when you seek me with all your heart," Jeremiah 29:13 NIV

Memorizing Scripture Takeaways:

- Reciting memorized Scripture is a love language. It shows who we love. It shows a priority. It's strategic spiritual coverage for our heart.

- Memorizing Scripture helps grow our faith. It's helpful to have in our mind to pull upon, recite, keep focused on what's important during life challenges and bring hope.

- Three Steps to Memorize Scripture: 1) Pick a verse you connect with. 2) Use visual cues to help remember. 3) Practice reciting.

Spiritual Insight

Some signs are clear. Others are for us to recognize and interpret. This is called spiritual insight. God transforms our limited vision through our spirit, being tuned to the Holy Spirit.

<u>Definition: Tune</u> (verb) To adjust to the frequency of the required signal, adjust to for precise functioning, to become attuned.

It's important to understand the need to form, develop, and deepen our spiritual relationship so that we can move into the next level of having spiritual insight. It's a building up process. We need a strong base to receive spiritual insight.

Spiritual insight, also called discernment, is knowing the message.

Spiritual insight is an internal process. It's slow and steady. It's developing our spiritual health, our spirit, our inward, in order for outward experiences to be known. The more you put into it, the more you get out of it. That is the equation of faith. The secret sauce of faith is our own inner reward.

Spiritual discernment can be often be a feeling. "I feel pulled to do this." But it's not clear why. It takes doing the message received to grow and gain deeper levels of spiritual insight.

Insight can be knowing why something happened in the past; understanding in hindsight. Another powerful position is when we have foresight; knowledge in advance. This is important so we focus our time, attention, and effort on the right priorities today, being ready for what comes in the future. It's being prepared.

Insight is knowing the steps God wants taken now. Today. It's not a 'whenever you get around to it' invitation. There is an urgency. It's pressure from within (your spirit, your heart, your soul) that does not fade. Spiritual insight for actions you need to initiate isn't always comforting. Why? Because it requires you to follow His way. This one requires courage and sacrifice in order to accomplish.

Insight is also knowing when we are being shifted, transitioning into a new season, and when we must to let go in order to move forward. This involves change.

When I've talked about spiritual insight, people have commented to me "that is hard." That it is hard to have discernment. No. No, it's not. It just requires something from you. What is it? For you to know. And for you to know the message requires 1) your time and 2) your developed and deepened internal, personal, 1:1 spiritual relationship. And that is not *hard*. You just have to put in the time. It's free. But still a lot of people don't do it.

Insight is a developed skill. It takes patience and perseverance and time to think deeply. It's not a quick win. The more you do it, the easier it becomes.

It's the same analogy with our personal health. Do you want to be fit externally? If yes, you put in the time. You pay attention to what you eat, to what you put into your body. You develop a discipline to workout, exercise, to gain physical strength. No one can do it for you. If it's important, you make it a priority. Same with our spiritual health. It's you.

Here's what is hard in the equation of spiritual insight. So, you want to know the message? What is the will of God for your life? Well, are you willing to do it? Now, that is the harder part. Like ideas, it's easy to have them; it's work to implement them. Like faith, it's easy to say we have it; but do you trust and believe when it's not your plan? Like insight, it's easy to say you want to have it; but when a knowing is received, will you take the required action to do it? Will you do the work to accomplish it? If you favor your comfort, your stable financial security, your certain life, and solid plans, the odds are not likely. Faith is easy when you only follow your way. God tests. People resist, Acts 7:51: "You stiff-necked people, uncircumcised in heart and ears, you always resist the Holy Spirit. As your fathers did, so do you."

God gives insight only when we get close and develop a strong personal, spiritual relationship. "This is why I speak to them in parables, because seeing they do not see, and hearing they do not hear, nor do they understand." Matthew 13:13

Some who have said to me that spiritual discernment is hard are from longtime believers and church going people. Again, I'm not against church, but many times people get stuck in a structured approach of external faith, in "going to" church, and either inadvertently miss, or choose to skip, the all-important requirement of faith. Which is, (say it with me aloud:) our internal, individual, personal, 1:1 spiritual relationship with God. I missed it growing up going to church and I know I'm not the only one.

What is Required for Spiritual Insight?

1. Building a Spiritual Foundation

There is a hunger within our spirit. Do you know it exists? It craves spiritual things. Prayer to connect. Stillness to hear. Gratitude to feel (heart). Scripture to grow (heart). Bible to see and know (heart to mind). Individually each spiritual habit carries impact. When applied in unison, there's a multiplying force — a divine power.

To receive spiritual insight we don't get to skip over the building block process. Opening the way to spiritual insight requires a strong foundation of spiritual discipline. Discipline is simply establishing a routine, prioritizing it, and repeating it. It's the detailed 5 Steps to Develop Your Spiritual Relationship, recap below:

1: Pray
2: Be Still
3: Be Grateful
4: Read the Bible
5: Memorize Scripture

2. Time

This is our one-to-one time with spiritual connection to the Holy Spirit. Internal, individual, solo time to know God's voice. It's a partnership. All good relationships require an investment of quality time. More, not less. More time is better.

It's not a quick fix. It's not a pill to pop for instant relief. It's a time devotion. We take time to deepen our spiritual relationship, so we can then depend on our faith to direct our thoughts, steps, and actions. Deep and wide. The secret sauce of faith is our own inner reward. Opening the way to spiritual insight requires our 1:1 time.

3. Being Open

This means not being closed off, not closed to what you haven't considered, thought or planned. Not locked into your way. Being open-minded is being willing to receive the spiritual message *and* take concerted action. This requires change and an openness to be moved externally.

Transitions are change and move us from our current spot. Transitions open the way for God to lead us farther and show us more. Most people don't like change. Why? We like structure, surety, support. Change requires new, different, and uncertain. People often prefer present surroundings to an unknown future. "I know what *this* is. I don't know what *that* will be." Transitions are a period of shifting. They aren't easy. They don't feel good because there is a stretching process when we grow. Connection point: Nature. God visually shows us what is required through the shifting of seasons, also known as transitions. As the photos within this book illustrate, movement and change is required for growth.

Transitions include: 1) Pruning — things and/or people removed. 2) Additional sowing/tending/watering/weeding — more years of work before harvest. 3) Waiting — it takes longer than expected for the blooming season. Here is where we develop more patience and perseverance. We prepare in extended seasons. Being open to transitions requires trusting God. "For I know the plans I have for you, says the Lord, plans for welfare and not for evil, to give you a future and a hope." Jeremiah 29:11

Look what God can do when we open ourselves. As an example, my education and background is business and human resources working in companies. I don't have training in photography. Writing was not an interest, nor a desire of mine. In fact, fifteen years ago I would have thought that was the worst thing ever. Why? I was moving too fast. In my offtime, my passion was road cycling. A good friend called it obsession. Well, passion and obsession is a fine line. I lived cycling. I loved cycling. Until I didn't. What was once so rejuvenating, for eight years, came to a close. Within, I knew I was done cycling. Intuition called for change, a slower pace — to go for walks instead of intensively train and compete. It was a shifting season to let go of cycling. I haven't ridden since. I haven't wanted to; it's not in me any longer. Hindsight: If I never stopped cycling, I would not have taken photos or become an author. Why? 1) Pace: I was going too fast. 2) Time: Cycling filled my schedule. There is a dual purpose with the requirement of time. It's our time to be (stillness). And our time to be available (seek). When cycling, I had no time and wasn't open. If we are already filled, how can anything new come in? God doesn't compete. We have to make space for and provide an opening.

The requirements of time and being open coordinate for receiving spiritual insight. Having an open spirit is not being closed-minded to how we spend our time. When we connect with the higher power, the Holy Spirit, God opens our eyes and opens a way. When we are open, we can see a new, different path. When we stay focused on our wants and comforts, we can miss seeing and knowing His higher plan. Opening the way to spiritual insight requires being open.

"How do you know if it's God's will?"

You will know it, when you seek it. And to seek it, you have to be *in* it. That's reading it; the playbook is the Bible. How else do you know a game plan? The greatest motivational speaker is the Bible. The grand life strategy is the Bible. Where do you receive your cues? From what everyone else is doing? No. How else will you know the way? "Follow me."

How do you know? It's in prayer. It's in stillness. "Be still and know." Did you catch that sequential order? To know comes after stillness. We know God's will by deepening our spiritual relationship.

Ask. Seek. Knock. These three action words seem simple, but it's not as easy as it sounds. It's straightforward, but then you get into it, you realize that just asking for something doesn't come. What are you asking for? Something you want? Something in your plan? Something in your control? Well, buckle up, and put on your game face, because that's not how the play of a faithful life works. If serious, you will be tested. It will take time. Who are you for? Your way? Your will? "Thy Kingdom come; Thy will be done," from The Lord's Prayer informs in Matthew 6:9-13. This phrase bubbles up in my mind, because it's in me. Memorized from reciting it year after year while growing up going to church. See, in God's plan, nothing is ever wasted.

Myth: "You'll have a sense of peace."

When God gives you something to do, when he shifts you, when he leads you on a different path, you most certainly will not have inner peace. Why?

Because it stirs your soul up. It gives your spirit marching orders before you know what steps to take. You don't understand why. It doesn't logically make sense in the world order we've constructed. You are being pushed and stretched and it doesn't feel good because it is out of your comfort zone. "Yipes" is the inner feeling. I've felt it many times. If you follow his leading, you will feel vulnerable. But inner peace does come. When? Once you finish the assignment. One done. Get ready for the next.

> **Spiritual insight is a path of nuggets and nudges to be discovered, uncovered and worked. This awakens our inner spirit, generating spiritual vitality.**

To illustrate this point, when starting, I didn't know about this *Soul Speaking* book. I didn't know I would be on this path ten plus years later. It's hidden within us. For us to seek and find. Jeremiah 33:3:

"Call to me and I will answer you, and will tell you great and hidden things which you have not known." To uncover the "hidden things" we have to overcome doubt.

Overcoming Doubt

One of the hardest things to do in life is overcome doubt — our own, from others, and from the Enemy. This is where the depth of our personal, internal spiritual relationship with God will determine our ability to step out on faith. Do you know God's "voice" within you? Can you hear your soul speaking? If not, how will you be able to step out on faith? It's easy to *say* you have faith. But what about when you are being asked to do something new? Will you recognize it? Will you discount it? Will you override your soul speaking voice? Do we look away, discount spiritual nuggets, signs and promptings? It can often be preferred to instead choose the logical, make-sense-of-it, "worldly" mind. It's hard to follow the unknown, the uncertain, and the uncomfortable road. Faith leads the way and brings peace when we get on the path which we have to uncover. The Holy Spirit provides clues, for us to seek, in order to find that which is hidden within us.

The deeper challenge of faith is the ability to trust. To believe. Taking action and following where God leads is a process. A direct outcome of trust is that our faith is deepened and we build confidence, which turns into courage. And courage is required to follow faith and bring out our idea — the "it"— within.

Overcoming doubt. Note the tense: -ing. It's a verb. It's a continuing process of action. Not a "one and done." The good news is this action gets easier with practice (when we work our idea and listen to the Spirit leading) because courage is developed.

"Be strong and of a good courage." Joshua 1:9

Divine Guidance

Do you recognize what God is giving you to think upon? Passions within. What you naturally see (a hole, a gap) that others don't. A thought pops into your mind. Does it keep calling you? Is there a pattern?

God works in big and small ways. Like when that job you've been looking for just works out. It's smooth. You didn't have to control it. You were steady and it came.

Small things, coincidences, or perfectly timed events are often easier to overlook or discount, but these are some of the most significant ways God communicates with us. It happens on a regular basis. When we take time to hone our spiritual relationship, insight is received through these nudges, signs and "just-so-happened" moments. Insight allows us to recognize them, feel the divine comfort, and know it as Holy guidance. It is soul speaking, soul stirring and spirit uplifting.

It wasn't until I deepened and grew my personal faith relationship that I started taking photos and writing about faith. I never wanted to be an author nor writer. But my soul always knew. "Why of course, Amy." I just had to get connected with my inner spirit and coupled with the Holy Spirit. It's a powerful combination. Because now it is so natural. It fits and flows. That's when you know it's from the divine Creator. He is quite creative in his ways. Have you noticed?

There's divine uniqueness in our light within, given from the all-knowing Creator above, which could even turn into a calling.

Soul Seeking and Speaking

I didn't know my soul was hungry until I fed it. Feeding it was listening to my inner voice. My spirit. It's not enough to pray and hear. We have to do. Taking action brings deeper spiritual insight. Moving externally on what's within us internally.

Prior I had a searching, a wanting, for an intimate relationship and thought somehow that would fill me within. It never provided.

It was only my personal, internal faith relationship that brought me a filling, a soothing, constant love. Wholeness and holy.

How an intangible, spiritual, faith pursuit can be the real, firm substitute. It's a contrast of the worldly things we acquire, can touch, can have, can consume, can get more of, can be shown, can be seen, where your mind thinks it's something more than what it really is.

When it's the invisible, internal, inward, unknown to others that provides substance, sustenance — a steady, sustaining presence. Full. We don't need a touch from a human person, we need to touch our spiritual, higher power. To get in touch with our personal internal, relationship with God. It's all right there within our reach, we just have to open the door.

From The Heart

God intends to communicate with us through our eyes, heart and spirit. When our heart and spirit are aligned, God opens our eyes to help us see. There are ample verses focusing upon our heart and spirit. Further, a divine correlation with our eyes. Why yes, a photo book.

"the precepts of the Lord are right, rejoicing the *heart*; the commandment of the Lord is pure, *enlightening the eyes*;" Psalm 19:8

"You shall therefore lay up these words of mine in your *heart and in your soul*; and you shall bind them as a sign upon your hand, and they shall be as frontlets between your *eyes*." Deuteronomy 11:18

"Give me your *heart*, and let your *eyes observe* my ways."
Proverbs 23:26

"having the *eyes* of your *hearts enlightened*, that you may know what is the hope to which he has called you, what are the riches of his glorious inheritance in the saints," Ephesians 1:18

"But, as it is written, "What no *eye* has seen, nor ear heard, nor the *heart* of man conceived, what God has prepared for those who love him," 1 Corinthians 2:9

"For the word of God is living and active, sharper than any two-edged sword, piercing to the division of *soul and spirit*, of joints and marrow, and discerning the thoughts and intentions of the *heart*." Hebrews 4:12

"Create in me a clean *heart*, O God, and put a new and right *spirit within* me." Psalm 51:10

"A new *heart* I will give you, and a new *spirit* I will put within you;" Ezekiel 36:26

Natural Movements

Nature leads the way, by design. Trees showcase this best in seasons. Between time, moving from one state to another, embracing change. To shift, let go, release, rest, to bud and grow.

Seasonal emphasis on point – from this to that. Change occurs within plants and trees before we notice the external change in appearance. Closings, endings, moving into the next stage for openings, new, and fresh growth.

Walking

Walking helps one think clearly. Move to be moved within. The natural action stimulates our brain, circulates blood and brings oxygen to open our mind and thinking process. The rhythm of walking, left-right motion, allows the bubbling up from internal recesses. Forgotten thoughts move to the surface, long held ideas rise up. Studies show walking is a catalyst for creative thinking and cognitive function. I often write while walking, using my phone's note app.

A long-held discovery by philosophers and writers is a link between deep, intuitive thinking with walking and writing. Move in order to be moved. God wants to move within us to then move us externally in action.

Photo right: Out for a walk this naturally formed smiley face was on the path. We see what we feel within. Have you noticed?

When externals align to the internal beat of your heart. | Autumn

—

"Methinks that the moment my legs begin to move, my thoughts begin to flow." —Henry David Thoreau, American writer, philosopher & naturalist. (1817-1862)

Faithful in the Smalls

An internal focus of gratitude expands how you see. It compliments faith. Add prayer and you've got a great start to the day.

Small things are big. The smalls done with consistency compound. What do you focus on and upon?

Story to illustrate the point and this photo: If I didn't share the early Everyday Cross photos that caught my eye, along with writing what I interpreted as the spiritual message in the image, I wouldn't have created and published my first book, *In Plain Sight,* years later. Years later. And if I hadn't done that first book, I would not have created, completed, and published the second, then third book and here is number four. Faith is a stepping process.

Being faithful in the small before knowing the big —a book!

"He who is faithful in a very little is faithful also in much; and he who is dishonest in a very little is dishonest also in much." Luke 16:10

Movement in seasons — as God shows us.
Winged seeds from trees, helicopters, take flight. | Spring

Believe It

One of the hardest things to do in life is overcome doubt — our own, that from others, and especially that placed by the Enemy. To step out on faith with that little idea within you.

When it doesn't make sense. When it's not what you've always done. When it's different from what others do. And when you don't know the outcome. Getting out of our comfort and control zone takes faith. Step by step.

Little steps accumulate. Consistency compounds. Over time our faith and our work grows— becoming deeper, bigger, like that mustard seed of faith. God gets us started and with work it naturally evolves and grows.

- What could you do if you really believed?
- Believed in what you are led to follow?
- Believed in God's voice, promptings, and nudges?

I believe if I'm meant to write, then God will give me the words. When we step out on faith God grows it. Every day is the right time and season for belief.

"And Jesus said to him, "If you can! All things are possible to him who believes." Mark 9:23

In every season, faith is full of plantings. | Winter

A Rising Voice

This is how we want God to speak to us, to make his plan known. Big. Bold. Unmistakable. A large sign. "Make sure I know it's from You; make sure it's clear."

But that's not always how God works. He works in the smalls too. The glorious, small, quiet, subtle, nuanced ways. How will we know?

Get quiet to notice. Be still to hear. Get close to know. Take time to see. Slow down your pace. We know in our spirit through the Spirit. We recognize God's communication channels when we have a developed relationship with God. Like any good, trusting, two-way relationship, that requires time, patience, and effort.

This photo is how we want God to communicate with us, how we want discernment to know his will— big, bold. But it's really a speck of light. A fleck. A glimmer. But you know what? It is so bright. It is a beacon. A guiding light. You know it clearly. You know his voice, be it by visual signs, repeated messages, subtle promptings, or simply an inner knowing because you know him through dedicated and devoted prayer. And he knows you. Our spirit knows because it's a rising voice within us, like this sunrise, a natural movement.

Don't only wish for big because God often works in the smalls. There is power in the smalls. Small steps accumulate. Daily habits build when done consistently. God likes to grow things. Doesn't everything start as a seed—the seed of an idea?

"And the Lord said, "If you had faith as a grain of mustard seed, you could say to this sycamine tree, 'Be rooted up, and be planted in the sea,' and it would obey you." Luke 17:6

Morning moves. | Autumn

Letting Go To Move Forward

Spiritual development brings shifting seasons and transitions, times when we need to let go in order to move forward. One of these areas is to let go of unmet expectations so we don't harbor resentment or become bitter. Reframe your mindset with these 2 words: Then Don't.

Two reasons these are freeing and help switch the perspective is because they 1) Release others and 2) Release you. There is no hold.

- Release others: Let your expectations go. Let go of what it was, what could've been, what should have been, or what it wasn't. The who, the what, or wondering why this happened. Let it go.

- Release yourself: Let go of the control. From what you self-imposed of an external factor (person). There is no hold.

People will or people won't. People will do what they say they will do or they won't. When people won't, God will. When people don't, God does.

Two words to reframe your mindset and let go of unmet expectations from others: Then don't. Two words: God does.

Nature leaves clues. Fall is a transitional time to reflect.
Be like the trees and what you need to drop — let it go. | Autumn

Benches For Rest

Benches provide a break between movement, a respite between efforts, a time to pause. Rest is important for our spirit, mind and body. We need breaks for spiritual rejuvenation. To revive. Benches are a subtle reminding symbol of this need.

In well-designed spaces, benches are placed strategically to offer a sit, a rest. Often, we find them placed around trees and natural elements as another signal of extra relief to our soul and inner spirit.

Mother Nature leaves clues and cues. Seasons show us the need to rest, to shift our focus. The release of leaves to let go and transition. Winter to rest and renew for spring to produce new growth.

Do you take time to rest? To pause between movement? Seasonal changes offer a welcoming pause to rest and reflect.

A new season also signals the requirement of change. A shift and transition in order to grow. Trees are a great example to illustrate this natural transformation. Glorious leaves full of fall color must be shed, branches become bare, removed from what they once firmly held, so that it is ready for the future of fresh spring buds. Preparing within. Working. Waiting. Pruning.

Trees are known by their fruit. What are you known for? What have you and are you producing?

Yellow carpet. Nature's exterior design;
Ginkgo leaves. | Autumn

Rest Brings Restoration

Words given to me by my father: "Rest brings restoration."

Have you ever received a few words that bring an immediate change in perspective? These did for me. In the summer of 2007, after a cycling accident brought many weeks of forced downtime from my active lifestyle, my patience was tested. While visiting, I asked my Dad for some words, literally. I said: "Dad, I need some words." as I stood on crutches in the kitchen.

Without hesitation, sitting at the kitchen table, he said: "Rest brings restoration." Just like that. These three little words soothed me. These words calmed my impatience. These words transformed the time of waiting into a greater purpose. Not just one of repair, but something more, a deeper healing to renewed, restored, regenerated, revitalized.

"Rest brings restoration." - Bill Bretall

His words gave me an immediate shift in perspective— a move to an understanding that you can't rush the healing on your time table. Wait and it will be given. A bigger movement. My broken hip bone was stronger when healed. Fused in strength. When we are broken, it's our spiritual mindset that makes the difference to bring us to a place of strength. So, no more was I rushing time. My Dad's words allowed me to see something bigger. Rest brings restoration. All in three words. The little things in life are big.

Sensory subtleties speak to the soul. | Spring

There's Always A Bright Spot

It can be longer than you thought it would take.
It can be harder.
And what if it doesn't work out?
There's always a bright spot. Find it.
Look for faith to lead the way.
When life is challenging, look for the good.
Shift your mind to see it and know it.

What calls to you?
What makes you feel alive?
What does your inner voice say?
What makes you feel?
What brings you energy? Do more of that. It's a signal.
It's up to each of us to find our inner light and bring it out into the world to shine for others.

Photo Right: Same time in the morning as the photo on prior page, but a different season brings different lighting.

The Spirit is subtle. We have to be intentional, attuned to notice it. Like a subtle shifting of morning light — the pink, the softness — so does our spirit lead us into deeper meaning and connection to follow, to be led, to be moved. Letting our spirit, connected to the Holy Spirit, be our guide.

A study published in Nature found that just taking note of one's environment can enhance creative thinking. | Summer

Winter

Spring

Summer

Autumn

Take Your Shot

Don't let it pass you by. The "it" of now. The it of your idea. The it of what if. The it of your purpose.

Using the photography analogy: It's not always going to be there—the photo, the feel. Landscapes change, light shifts, timing can't be fabricated.

Take your shot now because you can't go back to yesterday. Time: and all of a sudden a year, or years, have gone by. Coulda, woulda, shoulda.

The "it" will pass you by unless you take action. Step out on faith. Trust in your signs, spiritual nudges, and divinely timed nuggets on your path.

Photos Right: I didn't plan to have all four seasons of this tranquil setting. On walks I was drawn to this nook with the lovely trio of tall trees and bench. Taken over a two-year period, it wasn't until looking through my phone library several years later that I realized I had all seasons in this spot and view. Sometimes the bench was moved and I would scoot it back into the "right" position, where it belonged, centered with the tree trunk.

"This is the day which the Lord has made; let us rejoice and be glad in it." Psalm 118:24

Trees are a symbol of healing, growth and are grounding, helping revitalize and restore our roots = spirit.

Contrast

Don't Wait to Take Your Shot

Photo right is twenty-one minutes later than the photo on the following page.

These two photos illustrate the point of action and taking your shot. Which one draws you in?

The *Opening A Way* photo with the glorious clouds reaching above the trees and hill horizon caught my attention at the beginning of my walk at 7:23 a.m. Photo right was taken on my return at 7:44. I took this second photo only because of the stark contrast and takeaway: it visually illuminates inaction. A contrast of change. What a difference time can make — 21 minutes. 1,260 seconds. Same setting. Pretty much the same day. Photo right, without the clouds, doesn't elicit the same feel as the photo on the next page. It misses the mark.

The happenstance positioning and timing we often walk into, not recognizing the moment. Not observing the opening. Missing an opportunity when we don't act. Being content to let time escape. Unaware of the significance of our surroundings, the glorious glimpse we get to see. Don't wait to take your shot.

Compare and contrast this photo with the next page. | Summer

Opening A Way

Life is about finding our way. It's different for each of us. Our spirit, being connected to the Spirit, is a guiding gift. How we see our surroundings, interpret external happenings, develop the ability to shift our perspective, filter the negatives, to recognize what is for us. For us to do. For us to become. It's a continuous motion.

The photos in this book are about movement. Seeing the subtle shifts of seasons to open the door of an idea. Feeling the call within to advance it. Taking steps of faith to move forward. Letting go of things that are not in our best interest. Keeping our pace to advance. Taking a needed rest to pause and renew. Connecting to our spirit to hear our soul speak. Will we listen? Will we follow? Read page 146 for a reconnecting recap of the themed photo collection with additional questions to go deeper.

Life is how we choose to see it. Can we reframe the external and channel our internal in a positive direction? Curves, unexpected dips and re-routes are certain. What will we use to lead us? Our spirit informs us. Let the Holy Spirit be the guide for direction.

"But you shall receive power when the Holy Spirit has come upon you;" Acts 1:8

The mark you leave is yours to make. | Summer

Repeating Patterns

Patterns provide peace. God speaks to us through patterns. Repeating messages. Over and over. What do you notice? What catches your attention? What makes your soul stir? What makes you feel alive?

Take time to be still. To listen. To hear. To see. God utilizes all of our senses to communicate with us. The spirit leads, but only if we listen. Pray so you can know. Remove yourself from external noise sources to hear within. The sound of silence speaks to our soul so that we can go deeper. Our spirit is a felt-perception mechanism. It feels good when activated. Are you attuned to it?

"The Lord has given us eyes to see with and ears to listen with." Proverbs 20:12

A prayer: Lord, help me do what You've given me. Help me use what You've gifted me. Help me to know what You've placed before me. Help me walk into Your plans. Help me to walk in Your ways. Help me glorify You. Help me become who You made me to be. In all thy ways.

Do you see your repeating patterns? | Summer

Narrow Focus

Narrow it down to accomplish your goals— your why.

Don't get distracted. Say No. You don't have time for everything. Protect your time.

Not sure what you should focus on?

- Pray. Prayer provides clarity, helping you see and know where to spend time. Prayer leads you forward making it easier to narrow your focus.
- Take action. Doing helps you learn your why. Taking action in your idea, your purpose, your call, makes it easier to eliminate distractions that disrupts progression.

A focal point helps us see clearly and know it intently. Faith helps zoom in to stay on track.

You know what the Bible says about focus? "Enter through the narrow gate. For wide is the gate and broad is the road that leads to destruction, and many enter through it." Matthew 7:13

Tunnel Vision. It's hard to see faith in life when you're away from it. Apart vs. a part. When it's not near, not part of a daily priority, it's easy to drift and lose sight. How close are you? | Autumn

A Lens of Faith

From fourth grade with the then new advancement of lenses turning dark in the sun called "Transitions," the back-to-normal coloring took hours.

Some rough teen years. Rough. "Transition" years. Don't we wish we could look back and tell our younger self: "Hang on, it's just a short season, it will get so much better." Because we know the future photos, contacts come and later Lasik.

It's like faith. As an adult when I'm in a season of transition, I think of God looking down saying "Hang on, it's just a short season. I've got this, it will get so much better." He sees; he has the future lens, so I keep working to develop my lens of faith.

It took me awhile to find my faith. I grew up going to church, but missed the internal element, which I've learned is the most important part of faith. My early 40s is when I found my personal faith in a non-traditional way while taking walks in nature. At a low in life, for over a year I was developing a one-on-one relationship with God. While praying and asking, I started seeing "Everyday Crosses" —those formed in the unformed. Finding these natural cross images, I knew they were timed and placed for me, with the spiritual message: "I *see* you, Amy. Keep going."

Seeing life through a lens of faith.

God transforms our limited vision through our
spirit, shifting our perspective to see
his angle — the bigger picture.

Will You Bring Out Your Idea?

This is the photo that stirred my soul and got me to do something with a few of my cross photos. Title: Crossing the Road.

I kept looking at this particular photo. It spoke to me. I thought about it. There was an intuitive pull. Has this happened to you? Maybe not a photo, but the idea, the source of inspiration. It draws you in. You can't really explain it, other than it calls to you from within, stirring your spirit— it's what I call *Soul Speaking*.

<u>Backstory</u>: I landed on the idea of greeting cards because I like sending them. It was February, 2016. I had visited my cousins in Colorado, stopped along the drive and took this photo. When I returned home to Kansas City, I sent a card as a thank you for staying with them several days. I had recently started taking photos of crosses, seeing them in places I never noticed before. Because of this, I wanted to send a card with a cross. At the store, I was disappointed to only find sparkly, white Baptismal, or pastelly Easter-themed options. No. I wanted real, authentic crosses, not a made-up, graphical representation. During this time I was at a low in life and connected with a real cross; it knew my pain and provided comfort. There was a hole in the card market. A few months later the idea popped into my head: "Amy, take some of your cross photos and turn them into greeting cards." It was divine timing, from the Architect Above, that brought me to this intersection and product choice — a start point.

In this faith-driven journey, I realize that taking action on this idea would lead me on a different path I'd still be on ten years later. This is how God works. He starts with the small and likes to grow, expand, and evolve within us. Planting the seed of faith, the seed of an idea.

Discover what's been hidden in you. Will you follow the nuggets? Will you work the starting idea?

Crossing the Road. Or not? Will you?

Will your idea remain a photo in your phone?
Hidden. Unseen by others. Not shared.

Bring out what *is* within you.
Live your inspiration.

His Sight. Our Insight.

God sees us. Individually. He observes. Even when we aren't attuned, God is there. Always waiting to catch our attention. Do we slow down and make space to recognize Him?

God sees our pain. He takes notice and works for our good. Even when it may not seem like it. "God— I need help now." His view: "I see you. I'm here." God has a schedule we can't see. We can't rush the timing. It's for our belief, our trust— which is the outcome of our personal, spiritual relationship. His eyes watch our faithfulness. He knows our heart, our spirit.

Yes, "for we walk by faith, not by sight," as read in 2 Corinthians 5:7. But God utilizes our eyes as a vehicle of communication. It's the process of being inwardly attuned to achieve insight and outwardly alert through visual observation. Our eyes are a powerful sensory organ, deep with intentional design, noticing subtleties, always sensing, absorbing, even when we don't consciously comprehend. Divine power is gained through our inner spirit, connected to the Holy Spirit, for us to receive knowledge of hidden things— to see, sense, know, and discern through spiritual insight. It's for us to discover our *Soul Speaking*.

Photo: Opening eyes to the surrounding presence of divine signs, an Everyday Cross from *In Plain Sight: Faith Is In The Everyday*.

My Faith Background

You may be wondering about my faith background. I grew up going to Methodist church, but missed the most important part of faith—the internal, personal, spiritual relationship with God.

Going to church every Sunday was an expectation of my parents. We attended as a family. Even when I didn't want to go, like in high school, some days I preferred to sleep in instead of attend early service (always the early service at 8:30 a.m.), I went. It wasn't optional. I have good memories going to church and we were active — my sister and I were acolytes, Confirmation, weekly youth group, singing, even played handbells for a while. Church was a good environment to grow up in; I'm thankful for it. In college I didn't attend. As an adult, I've gone to church for spurts of time. Following a divorce at the age of 29, it was a place I turned for comfort. It wasn't until my early 40s, during a low, that I discovered my internal, personal faith and developed a connection through my one-to-one time of spiritual disciplines. Thus far, in 9.5 years I've read the Bible four times, cover-to-cover, a different translation each time. Versions read in chronological order: Life Study Application, King James Version, New International Version, and Revised Standard Version-1952.

Over the years, routinely, I listen to sermons from several pastors, but I don't attend church. I have tried, but struggle to connect in the structured setting and consider it an external aspect of faith. For the community aspect of faith I'm connected with several people of strong faith who help. Because my spiritual health continues to mature, I remain committed to my individual worship time and spiritual disciplines as the priority. It's deeply fulfilling, enriching, spiritually sustaining and bears fruit. I believe if I'm meant to write, God will give me the words. This is book four.

With faith, I've learned everything counts. Nothing is wasted. There is a time and season for all things.

Photo Locations

For historical reference and remembrance. Times change, things get moved, or remodeled, but I sure hope those benches remain.

Twenty-seven of the 36 paired photo/writing pages are taken in Kansas City, Missouri during each of the years of 2021, 2022, 2023, 2024.

Kansas City, Missouri locations:
- Green doors, archway: Ewing and Muriel Kauffman Memorial Gardens: pages: 5, 7, 9, 13, 15
- Bridges, runrise, sidewalk: Brush Creek Trail near the Country Club Plaza: 31, 33, 35, 111, 115
- Benches, stairs: The Nelson-Atkins Museum of Art: 25, 27, 29, 121, 125, 124-127, 129
- Seasonal/misc.: 117; 142 in 2017
- Ginkgo leaves/bench: Southmoreland Park: 119
- Sky/hill, cloud sky/hill: Thies Park: 131, 133
- Ivy corridor: Ewing Marion Kauffman Foundation: 135
- The Vale Tunnel: Rock Island Trail, railroad converted to nature trail: 137

Other locations:
- Window: Washington National Cathedral, D.C., 2016: 10, 11
- Stained glass pew, tiled stairs: Palm Beach, FL, 2023: 17, 23
- Tree line in snowfield, LaMonte, Missouri, 2022: 113
- Crossing the Road, Victoria, Kansas, 2016: 141

Where nature is shown, the season is noted. As a nature lover I like knowing this; maybe you do too.

Acknowledgments

A deep thank you and appreciation to Kristi Tedrow for proofreading the paired photo pages and feedback on chapters. Kristi helped me see an angle I missed. I had a blind spot. Initially, in the writing chapters, I was so focused on the flow, key points, and backstory, but I didn't clarify the steps. Kristi suggested I share a 'how-to' approach, the specific steps I had taken, for readers to be able to follow and apply themselves. "Ah, yes!" She saw it and helped me improve this book. I was so close to the content and needed her external perspective, demonstrating how we help one another in life. Friendships can level us up; iron sharpens iron.

Backstory: Kristi and I met through our HR careers in 1998 when the company I worked for acquired the company she worked for. Traveling across the U.S., we collaborated and conducted employee meetings together. Even under these circumstances, her job was going away and mine wasn't, we became friends. God blends people in our lives and I'm grateful for this long-standing, deep friendship.

For Scripture, I selected the Revised Standard Version, (RSV-1952) as it's the Bible I recently finished. It holds special significance because it is my Dad's Bible, given to him when he was age 17 "from Mother and Father on March 1, 1959," per the inscription. His hands held it, used it. And now my hands hold it, reading from the same pages. Receiving. It's also my favorite Bible version thus far.

Did you notice the photography and sight wording throughout the book? Focus, angle, filter, lens, view, perspective, picture, reframe, take the shot. See, sight, clarity, viewpoint, clarify, blind spot, oversight, insight, observe, overlooked, hindsight, and illuminate. Some readers will notice, others may not, so I'm spotlighting it here.

>

Use what you've got.
Use what you've been given.
Use your gifts.

- Amy Bretall

We are created to use our natural gifts, that which is uniquely within us. Ideas are the easy part. Ideas need life. This means action, implementation, and work. Discover your it, bring out your idea, and start. Not sure? It's unknown and you are searching, needing more meaning in life? Pray. Prayer is the number one game changer in life. Prayer + action is a force multiplier.

<u>A reconnecting recap to the photography collection of movement:</u> Do you spiritually see the window of opportunity? Will you reach toward and grasp the handle to open the door? Or does a door need to be closed so you can move ahead? Will you walk through the archway leading you toward? Will you take the steps required? Will you step up? Will you continue to do the work? Will you take a rest to renew your spirit, mind and body? Will you recognize the season you're in? Will you change and transition, as nature divinely teaches, to stay on track? Will you take the bridge to continue advancing? Bridging the gap you may not even realize, but continue moving, being innately led by your inner spirit. Do you see the naturally formed openings before you? Can you feel your light within? Do you know it? Will you be open to letting yourself be led? All require action, our individual initiative. And our developed internal, personal, spiritual relationship. Let yourself be moved from the internal to the external. From your *Soul Speaking* inner spirit and connection to the Holy Spirit opening and leading the way.

Prior to becoming an author, photographer and faith-driven entrepreneur, Amy Bretall held senior-level human resources leadership positions during her 25+ years in the for-profit, private sector. Before starting her consulting company, Arbor Grove, in 2014, Amy was Senior Vice President, HR at Arvest Bank. Consulting, she worked with small, local businesses to large-scale global companies on strategic HR project direction, management, and business implementation. Amy received a B.S. in Business/Human Ressources degree from Missouri State University.

Transitioning from a successful business career into a faith-driven entrepreneur is a story of transformation and belief in God's leading. Amy's authentic story of overcoming doubt and how she stepped out on faith to create and publish a series of non-fiction Christian books, inspires others to see the signs of faith in everyday life. She lives in Kansas City, Missouri. Author photograph: Raye Jackson.

An accomplished photographer, using only the camera on her phone, Amy's work has been recognized and featured in multiple solo exhibitions including the First Fridays Crossroad Arts District in Kansas City, Missouri and state-wide publication, *Missouri Life*. Amy created a unique line of Christian inspirational products with her photography of crosses to uplift and keep the focus on faith at LiveBreatheAlive.com. Believing if she is meant to write then God will give her the words; *Soul Speaking* is Amy's fourth book. Follow along Amy's journey to see where it leads.

Learn more and sign up for her inspiring newsletter at amybretall.com. Connect: Instagram @amybretall, Facebook: @Live Breathe Alive

amybretall.com

Praise for Amy's Books

An Exceptional Devotional Book of Imagery and Inspiration
"Many people struggle to find evidence of God in today's world, but for Amy Bretall, the Divine is everywhere if we but open our eyes and hearts to God's presence. In Plain Sight teaches us to see the sacred in the ordinary through Ms. Bretall's extraordinary photos of crosses formed by cracks in the sidewalk, shadows on a wall, twigs on the ground. Her thoughts accompanying the many photographs take us on her own journey of faith as she uses the images to find meaning in her life. Bretall's inspirational words and photos will encourage the reader to look more closely at their own environment and examine their own life to discover God in plain sight." — **Shirley Gilmore, author of Bucky and the Lukefahr Ladies series,** | In Plain Sight

Authentic and Inspirational
"Amy's gift for seeing visual reminders of God's presence in the everyday world is a joyful reminder of God's constant presence. Her writing matches her visual style; authentic and inspirational. For me, her book's been a reminder that we can see God at work in the world every day, if we only slow down and look." — **Michael Turner, pastor** | In Plain Sight

Beautiful Book to Reignite Your Faith
"Amy has such a way of capturing a photo and then reminding you of the simplicity of the beauty that we often overlook. This is a great book to reignite your faith and hope in the moments of your everyday life. This book also makes a great gift for someone who may need to be reminded that their faith will see them through their struggles. Beautiful work!" —**Christina Jolly, Christian podcast Believe for Bigger** | In Plain Sight Vol. II

New Outlook in Life
"After my wife passed I was really down and wondered the meaning of life. I sure am enjoying life much more since reading your three books. I see things differently now and have a new outlook in life. These books have helped my faith. I never would have read those Scriptures if they weren't in your book." —**Charles S.**

A Magnificent Obsession
"Reading Amy Bretall's book of images of the cross *In Plain Sight* has some really beautiful images shot with her iPhone coupled with poetry and reflections. Amy has a "magnificent obsession" to see the cross in everyday life." — **Adam Hamilton, founding pastor, Church of the Resurrection**

Nurtures Spiritual Growth
"What an engaging book! I often miss seeing the wonders of God's creation. This book encourages me to look up at the clouds and within my soul to evaluate my relationship with God. In the book Amy honestly shares the journey of her soul during the process of producing fine work. Amy's writing and eye-catching photos help me to look up at the heavens with more awareness and to look within my soul to nurture my spiritual growth." — **Cliff Rawley, retired chaplain, Doctor of Ministry, Master of Divinity** | Sights of Faith

Beautiful & Meaningful Book
Gorgeous book. Not only are the pictures beautiful, but Amy's words are authentic, encouraging, and inspiring. I gave this book as a gift and it was a huge hit. Unexpected upside? I now see crosses everywhere and it makes me smile and give thanks every time. — **Lynn Price, bestselling author of Negotiate It!** | In Plain Sight

"Mundane-Made-Holy Scenes" — Missouri Life Magazine

A Journey of Self-discovery
"The images together with Amy's words are so beautiful and take you on a journey of self-discovery as it unravels the profound symbolism of crosses found hidden in the tapestry of everyday life." — **Kristi Ziegler, Interior Designer** | In Plain Sight Vol. II

Beautiful Work
"What a beautiful compilation of photos, poems, and Scripture. Beautiful work! I gifted this to my mom and it was a hit. Thank you for sharing your talent with the world, Amy!" —**Kara B.** | Sights of Faith

No matter where we are in our faith journey, there is always more to see.

Why? Because the Holy Spirit is always working.
Within us and through us.
To grow and shine our light to help others.

Also by Amy Bretall

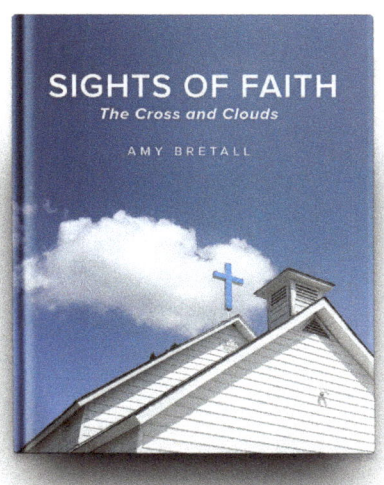

amybretall.com

www.ingramcontent.com/pod-product-compliance
Lightning Source LLC
Chambersburg PA
CBHW042043280426
43661CB00093B/979